D0099666

THE LABOR
RELATIONS PRIMER

THE LABOR
RELATIONS PRIMER

WESLEY M. WILSON, *B.S., M.B.A., J.D.*

 1973

DOW JONES-IRWIN, INC., *Homewood, Illinois 60430*

First Printing, July 1973

ISBN 0-87094-060-0
Library of Congress Catalog Card No. 73–80103
Printed in the United States of America

Preface

My goal in writing this book is to provide an introduction to the broad field of labor and employment law. The book, in which I have attempted to be objective in my analysis of labor law, is planned to be most helpful to businessmen who are also employers.

Few businessmen have time to maintain a working knowledge of the complex labor laws. Yet, if an employer is faced with demands from a union, for recognition or for a contract, for example, he must take proper action or risk being involved in costly hearings, court cases, or picketing or a strike.

In describing the structure and organization of the National Labor Relations Board, I have assumed that most readers have little understanding of this most important agency. I have attempted to explain what constitutes an unfair labor practice and what one should do to avoid committing a "ULP."

There is no intent to have this book substitute for professional legal counsel, but rather to give the reader the background necessary to understand what his labor law specialists advise. After studying this book, it is my hope that an employer can reduce his risks and improve his bargaining power. He will know what he can and cannot do, and what his employees or a union can and cannot do.

Yakima, Washington　　　WESLEY M. WILSON
June 1973

v

Contents

vii

Alphabetical listing of major topics

THE LABOR RELATIONS PRIMER

SUMMARY OF
FEDERAL AND STATE AGENCIES

There are many federal and state agencies and laws which apply to the rights of employees in dealing with their employer, their union, and others. This book will help employers and individuals to become aware of those rights.

The NLRB is an independent federal agency which administers the National Labor Relations Act of 1935, as amended by the Taft-Hartley Act of 1947 and by the Landrum-Griffin Act of 1959. The NLRB conducts elections to determine whether employees want a particular union to represent them or whether they want to get rid of the union which represents them, and it determines whether employers or unions have committed certain acts which are an unfair labor practice.

National Labor Relations Board

The U.S. Department of Labor, headed by the Secretary of Labor, a member of the President's Cabi-

U.S. Department of Labor

1

net, has many activities. They include the following:

1. Administration of the Wage and Hour Law and the Public Contracts Act; the Landrum-Griffin Act as it applies to controls over unions and their relationship with union members, the Welfare and Pension Plans Disclosure Act, and the Bureau of Veterans Re-Employment Rights.

2. Coordination of the state-federal public employment offices and unemployment compensation system, apprentice and other training programs.

3. Gathering, analysis, and publication of data about employment, earnings, and cost of living.

Railway Labor Act

This act applies to labor relations between railroads and commercial airlines and the unions which represent their employees. It established the National Mediation Board to handle "major disputes" and the Railroad Adjustment Board and airline systems boards to handle "minor disputes," such as arbitration matters.

Equal Employment Opportunities Commission

This independent agency was established under Title VII of the Civil Rights Act of 1964. It is managed by the five-member Equal Employment Opportunity Commission (EEOC). There are regional offices in various cities throughout the country. This act prohibits discrimination in hiring, laying off, promotions, transfers, and so forth, in employment on the basis of race, color, religion, sex, or national origin. It applies to employers with 15 or more employees, to labor organizations with 15 or more members, and to employment agencies.

Occupational Safety and Health Review Commission

This independent agency was established under the Occupational Safety and Health Act of 1970. The law requires each employer to furnish employment which is free from hazards likely to cause death or serious physical harm to his employees. It provides for establishing safety standards for industry, and for warning labels and posters. An employee or union agent can request that an agent of the Secretary of Labor visit the work area claimed to be unsafe, and if a hazard is found a citation may be issued and a penalty assessed if the hazard is not corrected.

About 17 states have a State Labor Relations Act **State laws** which applies to employers not covered by the federal National Labor Relations Act or the Railway Labor Act. These state acts usually provide for a state agency to conduct elections, and they prohibit certain unfair labor practices of employers, unions, or individuals.

Most states have laws requiring the payment of wages when an employee quits or is fired, the payment of an overtime rate under certain conditions, and laws restricting hours and days of work and the type of work which women and minors can do. All states have a law providing a form of insurance for employees injured on the job (workmen's compensation).

Many states have an agency with authority to administer a safety law similar to the federal Occupational Health and Safety Act. More than half of the states have laws prohibiting discrimination on the basis of race, color, national origin, sex or age.

HOW LABOR UNIONS ARE ORGANIZED

If employees are not represented by any labor union, some employees may desire to organize their own union, or to talk with agents of existing unions.

Unions are more successful in organizing where employees are not satisfied. Employees may believe that their employer pays lower wages than a competitor or lower wages than others in their area. Some employees may organize to get a "better" pension plan or health and welfare plan. Sometimes morale is low among employees because of too much overtime or too little work, or because of acts by management which employees believe to be arbitrary.

In the past, most labor unions tended to limit themselves to representing employees in a particular industry or to employees performing a particular type of work. In the past few years, however, many unions have been willing to represent many types of employees working for a broad range of employers.

Most union organizers will be glad to talk with an employee, or to meet with any employees. The organizer will probably meet with employees at the union office or in a private home, usually in the evening. In the meeting he will probably explain the procedure used by his union — how authorization cards or applications for membership in the union would be used, the procedure for getting recognition from the employer if enough employees are interested in that union, and the procedure in negotiating a collective bargaining agreement. He will probably pass out authorization cards, usually 3 x 5 inches in size, to employees and ask that they sign them.

The organizer will request that each employee present ask other employees to sign a card and return it to him or to one of the "key" employees helping him. The cards should not be signed on company property during working time, but they could be signed in nonworking areas during nonworking time such as coffee breaks or the lunch period. Some supervisors do not like any talk about a union and they may ask questions to determine who is trying to bring the union in. Many organizers tell employees not to discuss their organizing efforts with supervisors, or to let them know that there is interest in organizing a union.

If employees want to organize an "independent union" and not be subject to control by outsiders they can prepare authorization cards by a mimeograph machine or similar process. A model authorization card which could be used for an election or to seek recognition without an election appears on page 104. Or an employee can prepare a petition such as the following for any union, including an "independent union" which employees want to establish:

We, the undersigned employees of *John Doe Company*, desire that the National Labor Relations Board conduct an election to determine if the *John Doe Employee Union* should be our exclusive bargaining representative.

Signature: Date:

If employees organize an "independent" or "company" union they should choose a name and select a committee of fellow employees to establish a constitution and bylaws. They will want to decide what offices the union has, how officers are selected, the length of their terms, the amount of initiation fees and dues, when meetings will be held, and so forth. An employer and his supervisors should not participate in forming or operating a union, for they may be charged with an unfair labor practice.

If the union is recognized by an employer as the exclusive bargaining representative, whether or not it has won an election, the union must meet certain requirements of the Federal Labor-Management Reporting and Disclosure Act of 1959 (Landrum-Griffin Act). Within 90 days after recognition by an employer the union must file a report with the U.S. Department of Labor, Office of Labor-Management and Welfare-Pension Reports (LMWP). A union must adopt a constitution and bylaws and two copies must be filed with a report, Form LM-1. A union is required to list names of its officers, initiation and other fees, regular dues and other periodic payments required of members, and information such as:

Restrictions on membership;
How to participate in insurance or other benefit plans;
How disbursement of union funds is authorized;
How meetings are called;
How officers and others are selected or disciplined;
How fines or discipline of members are handled;
How hearings and appeals are handled;
How bargaining demands and strikes are authorized;
How contract terms are ratified; and
How work permits are issued.

The annual financial report requires listing of (a) assets and debts owed at the beginning and end of the year, (b) receipts and where they came from, (c) salaries and payments to officers and employees, (d) money paid out, (e) loans to any business, and (f) loans which totaled $250 or more in a year to any officer, employee, or member.

If the total value of the property and yearly receipts of the union is more than $5,000, then a bond to protect against loss by fraud or dishonesty must cover each officer, agent, shop steward, representative, or employee of the union who handles union funds or other property.

The regional office of the LMWP can help an individual in filling out the reports, but they must be mailed to: Director, Office of Labor-Management and Welfare-Pension Reports, U.S. Department of Labor, Washington, D.C. 20210.

Getting signatures Employees should not get signatures of other employees during working time. Soliciting signatures for the petition or cards can be prohibited in work areas, if the employer prohibits solicitations for charity fund drives or other groups. A foreman who may be a true "supervisor" rather than just a leadman or "straw boss" should not sign.

When 30 percent or more of the employees in an "appropriate bargaining unit" sign cards for the union it may send those cards or a petition with a "Petition" for an election form to a regional office of the National Labor Relations Board. The NLRB will then send a copy of that petition to the employer.

The appropriate bargaining unit

The NLRB will not order an employer to bargain with a union unless it claims to represent all employees in "an appropriate bargaining unit." Likewise, the NLRB will not conduct an election unless it covers employees in an appropriate voting unit. Most bargaining units cover "all production and maintenance employees." Some units, however, may include only a particular group of employees, who have a different type of work or hours, or working conditions much different from other employees, and who have separate supervision or a separate work location.

Some groups of employees which may be permitted to have a separate unit include truck drivers, warehouse employees, salesmen, laboratory employees, and maintenance employees in a "true craft unit" which usually requires an apprentice training period. Office clerical employees and professional employees (such as engineers, usually required to have an engineering degree) are excluded from an overall production and maintenance unit in most cases. Guards, watchmen, and supervisors are excluded in all cases. A "supervisor" is more than a leadman or "straw boss" but he may not have authority to hire or fire.

If an employer has several locations, each plant or store may be an appropriate unit. The NLRB usually "presumes" that a single plant or store can be an appropriate unit. However, if they are only a few miles apart, there is some transfer of employees from one location to another, and most management decisions are made at another location, then the NLRB may find that a separate unit is not appropriate. An individual can phone or visit the NLRB regional office nearest him for information about the appropriate unit.

Getting recognition from the employer
A union cannot be effective in getting improved wages, hours, and working conditions unless it is recognized by the employer as the "exclusive" bargaining representative for employees. (However, some laws covering government employees permit a union to represent and sign a contract only for its members.) A union which has authorization cards from over half of the employees in a bargaining unit will frequently write a letter to the employer requesting that it be recognized and that the employer meet with it to bargain for a contract.

Many employers will not accept such a statement and will either insist upon an NLRB election or other proof that the union represents the employees. Sometimes there is a "card check" by a neutral person such as the State Department of Labor. This "card check" consists of a comparison of the names and, perhaps, also the signatures on the authorization cards with a list of names submitted by the employer, and perhaps also the signatures of employees from the employer's payroll records. The person conducting the "card check" will then certify whether the union represents a majority of the employees, based upon the authorization cards.

Sometimes an employer will not agree to a "card check" or with the results of a "card check," and he will refuse to agree to recognize the union unless it wins an election. The NLRB usually upholds the right of an employer to insist that the union win an

election. But if the employer commits "serious" unfair labor practices (such as threats to fire employees
who support the union, or to close his business if
the union wins), then the NLRB may, after an unfair
labor charge is filed and a trial is conducted, order
the employer to bargain with the union without an
election, if it had authorization cards from a majority of the employees.

Sometimes the employer has reason to doubt
that the employees who signed an authorization card
really want the union to represent them. For example, there may be organizing activity by two or
more unions and the same employee may sign an
authorization card for each union. Sometimes a
union organizer tells employees that the card is to
be used only to get an NLRB election and says
nothing about the possibility that the card may be
used to seek recognition by the employer without
an election. Sometimes the language on the cards
is so confusing that the card does not clearly authorize the union to represent that employee for the
purposes of bargaining with the employer. The
union may request recognition in a bargaining unit
which the employer believes is not appropriate. For
example, the union may seek recognition in one department, and the employer may contend that only
a unit of all employees would be appropriate. In all
of those cases the NLRB may not order the employer
to bargain with a union, even though it had cards
from most of the employees. In any of these situations the employer may insist that the union file a
petition for an NLRB election, or the employer may
file a petition for an election.

NATIONAL LABOR RELATIONS BOARD
ELECTION PROCEDURE

If an employee wants the NLRB to conduct an elec-   **Petition form**
tion he must complete the NLRB's "Petition" form,

sign it, and send it to the NLRB regional office near him. The NLRB regional office will send him copies of their petition form and their agents will help him complete the form if the employee should ask them for help. There is no fee for this service. If an employee prefers he may consult a private attorney to assist him, and he will be expected to pay the attorney's usual fee. A list of addresses and phone numbers of the NLRB regional offices appears on page 99 and a completed copy of the NLRB petition appears on page 102.

Within 48 hours after filing the petition, but preferably with the petition, an individual or a union must also send to the NLRB proof that at least 30 percent of the employees in the proposed bargaining unit want the election. This could be union authorization cards recently dated and signed by the employee.

NLRB dollar jurisdiction requirements

The NLRB will not conduct an election or handle an unfair labor practice matter unless the employer involved meets the "jurisdictional standards" of the NLRB. A retail business must have gross sales of at least $500,000 a year to meet these standards. A non-retail business, such as a warehouse, factory, or contractor, in general, must either buy $50,000 a year worth of products from outside the state or do that much business a year with customers who do.

For a case against a union, the NLRB usually looks at the volume of business done by an employer involved in the matter against the union. For example, if the charge is that a union is not fairly operating a hiring hall, look for the business volume done by any employer who has an agreement to hire employees from that hall.

The NLRB regional office can advise the employee on its jurisdictional standards.

If employees want to get rid of a union which they do not like, any employee in the unit represented by the union may file a petition to "decertify" the union. See page 103 for a completed NLRB petition form. With the election petition or within 48 hours, the "petitioner" must send to the NLRB office recently signed and dated signatures from 30 percent or more of the employees in the bargaining unit. One way to obtain this "showing of interest" is for an employee to prepare a heading such as the following on a sheet of paper:

Decertification elections

We, the undersigned employees of_____
_____ Company, desire that the National Labor Relations Board conduct an election to determine whether the _____
_____ Union continues to represent the employees.

Signature: Date:

An employee should not circulate that petition for signatures in working areas during paid time, but he may circulate it during coffee breaks or during lunch periods, or before or after working hours. Do not get signatures of supervisors, and do not get prior approval of management before circulating the petition, since the union may claim that the employer has given unlawful assistance to the employee, and the NLRB may not conduct the election.

On the NLRB petition form under "Unit Involved" the petitioner should state the existing bargaining unit. If he does not know this and there is a recent collective bargaining agreement he can copy the job classifications listed there as "Included" and list the usual exclusions (guards and supervisors). One may phone or write to the nearest NLRB regional office to answer other questions about how to get an election.

(Note: the bylaws of some unions provide that a member may be fined by the union if he files a petition to decertify the union. If the union threatens to fine an employee for this reason it is an unfair labor practice; notify the NLRB.)

Union security elections

If an employee cannot file a petition to decertify the union because an election is "barred" by a contract, but he does not want to continue to pay dues or fees to the union, he can file for a "union security de-authorization election." "Union security" includes a contract requirement that employees join the union after 30 days (or after 7 days in the construction industry) or pay fees to the union. To get the election an individual must obtain signatures from 30 percent of the employees as stated above under "Decertification Elections." An employer cannot ask for this kind of election. On a sheet of paper an employee could prepare a heading such as the following:

We, the undersigned employees of _____
_____ Company, desire that the National Labor Relations Board conduct an election to determine whether the union security clause, section _____ in the collective bargaining agreement, should be removed.

Signature: Date:

In the NLRB petition form list the bargaining unit as provided above. The "petitioner" should also send to the NLRB a copy of the current bargaining agreement or the recently expired agreement, and mark the union shop, the agency shop, union dues checkoff, or other form of union security in the contract. If, in the election, a majority of the employees vote to remove the union security provisions of the contract, the NLRB will certify that the union security provisions are no longer effective. The remaining portion of the contract will remain in effect, but the union cannot then request the employer to fire anyone because he has not paid dues or initiation or other fees.

Where a union makes a claim upon the employer that it represents the employees, the employer may itself file a petition for an election with the NLRB. The employer may also petition for an election if he believes that the union with which he has been dealing no longer represents the employees, but with this petition he must sign a letter stating what facts cause him to doubt that the union represents his employees.

An employer may petition for an election

An employee should send an original and about three copies of the signed, completed petition form to the nearest NLRB regional office. One copy of the sheet with employee signatures, or of authorization cards, will be enough. The NLRB will "docket" the petition as a "case," assign it to a field examiner or attorney in the regional office and will send a copy of the petition to the company and to the union, if any. With the petition to the company, the NLRB will send a copy of a "Notice to Employees" form advising of the filing of the petition and of rights of employees, and ask that it be posted. The NLRB will also send to the company a form requesting information to determine if the NLRB has "jurisdiction" over the company.

What the NLRB will do with the petition

The NLRB will not usually conduct an election if there is a collective bargaining agreement currently in effect. This is called the "contract bar rule." However, the NLRB will accept the filing of an election petition in the 30-day period beginning 90 days and ending 60 days before the contract's expiration or "automatic renewal" date. If the contract is at least two years and nine months since its effective date, the NLRB will accept the filing of a petition by employees or a petition by a rival union, even though the contract by its terms still has another year or more to run.

The NLRB will not conduct an election for a full year after any prior "valid" NLRB election.

Agreements for an election

If the employer and the union and any other party "consent" to an election, they should sign a standard NLRB form agreeing that the regional director of the NLRB may resolve any disagreement as to whether there was improper conduct by either of them before the election, or whether particular individuals were eligible to vote. If an individual signs this kind of form, his right to appeal any action of the regional director is very limited.

Another type of form provides that the parties "stipulate" that if there are disagreements as to whether there was improper conduct or whether particular individuals were eligible to vote, that the regional director only makes an investigation and a report for the Board, which resolves the dispute.

Hearing to determine if election should be directed

If the parties do not sign an election agreement, the regional director will probably direct that a hearing be conducted to determine if there should be an election. That hearing is normally scheduled in the city where the employer's business is located, a few weeks after the petition is filed. Presiding at this hearing will be a hearing officer from the NLRB regional office; a court reporter will record what is said and later will type a transcript. If an individual files the election petition, he will probably want to be represented by an attorney. However, the hearing officer will assist him in seeing that an adequate record is made to properly resolve the issues in the case.

The hearing officer will ask the employer, the union, and any other party to enter into certain stipulations of fact and law. Among those are the type of and amount of business done by the employer, that the union is a "labor organization," that the filing of the petition raised a "question concerning representation," the history of bargaining by the employer with any union, and on the employees that should be included and excluded from the bargaining unit. Witnesses will then testify and exhibits will be received as evidence.

Decision of NLRB regional director

A month or so after the hearing closes, the regional director usually issues a written decision, either dismissing the petition, or directing that an election will be conducted in a particular unit of employees. He sends a copy of his decision to all parties to the hearing.

Election eligibility list

If the union and the employer consent to an election or if the NLRB directs that an election be conducted, the employer will be asked within seven days to file with the NLRB an election "eligibility list" of those employees who can vote in the election. The NLRB will send a copy of this list (often called the "Excelsior list," named for the case where the NLRB first issued this requirement) with names and the home addresses to all other "parties" to the election. The other parties may then use this list to send election campaign literature.

Election campaign propaganda and meetings

Before any NLRB election there is usually campaign propaganda put out by the union and the employer. Campaigns before an NLRB election are somewhat similar to campaigns before any national or state election.

The union usually promises that if employees select the union that it will negotiate a collective bargaining agreement for them similar to agreements which it or other locals of the union have negotiated with other employers. The union usually promises a wage increase, better health and welfare or pension benefits, and protection for employees against arbitrary action by the employer. Unions often try to convince employees that the employer will cheat them in every way he can, and employees need this union to protect themselves.

The employer usually states that employees presently enjoy wages and other benefits equal to that existing in other companies which have a union; that the union cannot promise and guarantee employees anything; if the union wins an election the employer will bargain in good faith but neither the union, the NLRB nor anyone else can force him to agree to anything. An employer may state that if he does not agree to union demands it may force the employees to strike, in which case the employees would not have any earnings and the employer could permanently replace them with new hires. The employer will point out (except in states with a "right to work law") that if the employees select a union it may negotiate a contract which will require that all employees join the union and pay monthly dues of a certain amount each month, that an employee who does not join the union will have to be fired and the union can fine employees if they violate the union's rules.

The union agents can meet with employees at their homes and attempt to get their support. The NLRB usually rules that it is not proper for an employer or supervisors to follow a practice of visiting employees in their homes to try to convince them not to support the union.

Supervisors and other employer officials may state their opinion to employees about the union in the location where employees work, or in a meeting with a group of employees.

If an employer holds a "captive audience" meeting with employees during paid time to discuss the union it may request a similar meeting to reply. The union may not be entitled to such a meeting if it can talk with a large portion of the employees during lunch or rest periods or in their homes or other places.

Over the years the NLRB has developed for its elections rules which are usually considered to provide for a fair election. The procedure varies slightly among the NLRB regions, but the procedure is substantially as given below:

Voting in NLRB elections

A few days before the scheduled time of the election, the employer should post on the bulletin board the NLRB's "Notice of Election" form, which states the voting unit, the date, time and place of election, and has a sample of the NLRB's secret ballot.

About half an hour or more before the time that balloting is scheduled to begin, the party who filed the petition (petitioner), the union(s), and the employer agents meet with the NLRB agent. He will ask the employer, union, and other parties to select one or more observers to help him to conduct the election. It is not necessary that any party have an observer, but he may if he wishes. An observer cannot be a full-time agent of the union or a supervisor or other agent for the employer. In this "preelection conference," the NLRB agent will explain the voting procedure and the parties will then inspect the voting area.

Shortly before the opening of the polls, the NLRB agent and any observers will have before them the list of eligible voters received from the employer. This usually lists employees who are on the payroll in a job in the bargaining unit during the payroll period which ended just before the election was directed or consented to. When the balloting begins each voter states his name to the NLRB agent. The observers check his name on the eligibility list, and the NLRB agent hands the voter a ballot. The voter then takes it to the nearby hidden area, such as an adjoining room or a booth, marks it, folds it and puts it into the ballot box and leaves the voting area.

In some elections there may be several voting periods. After each period the ballot box is sealed by closing the slot with tape and by writing signatures across the tape.

At the close of the balloting the polls are closed and the union, employer, and other parties are called back into the area for the count. The NLRB agent prepares a "Certification on Conduct of Election" form and asks the observers to sign it, certifying that all eligible voters had a chance to vote in secret. A party may later file objections to the election even though his observer signed this form.

Before the count is begun the NLRB agent attempts to get the parties to agree whether individuals whose ballot was challenged had the right to vote. Then the NLRB agent counts the ballots, with the parties observing. At the end of the count the NLRB agent prepares a "Tally of Ballots" and gives a copy to each party.

A sample ballot where only one union seeks recognition is included at page 105. The ballot used where two or more unions are competing is similar, but it also has a block for "Neither."

A union must have a majority of the valid votes cast to be certified as the exclusive bargaining representative of employees in the voting unit.

If there are two or more choices such as "no," and two or more unions, but no choice receives a majority, a runoff election may be scheduled between the two choices which receive the greatest number of votes. Those eligible to vote in the runoff election will be those employees who were eligible to vote in the first election, provided that they are still employed in the voting unit as of the date of the runoff election. Employees new to the voting unit will not be permitted to vote in the runoff.

Sometimes the NLRB will conduct an election by mail ballot or a combination of mail ballot and manual voting. Mail ballots are sent from the NLRB regional office to the homes of voters a week or more before the count. Instructions are sent with each ballot. A notice of election is posted at the employer's premises and the employees are informed that if they do not receive a ballot by a certain date they should immediately ask the NLRB for a copy if they believe they are eligible to vote. If an individual filed the petition and believed that someone may vote whom he believes not to be eligible to vote, he should phone or write a note to the NLRB agent stating that he wants to challenge that person's vote, and the reason for the challenge. The parties are notified that they may be present for the count, at a stated time and place, usually in the regional office of the NLRB.

Mail ballot elections

If the number of challenged ballots which are not resolved could affect the outcome of the election then the election is usually not final until the NLRB rules on whether each individual whose ballot was challenged had a right to vote.

Challenged ballots and objections

Within five calendar days, beginning the first day after the election and ending at the close of business of the fifth day, any party may file objections to the conduct of the election. Objections must be postmarked before midnight. Four copies must be mailed to the NLRB regional office and a statement added such as the following:

I hereby certify that on this date I served a copy of the above objections upon (names and addresses of all other parties, such as the employer and the unions or petitioner) by depositing a postage prepaid copy addressed to each of the above parties.

Signed this _____ day of _____, 19____.

The objections must state exactly what you think another party did which was wrong and which interfered with the conduct of the election, or the right of employees to express their free choice. One may object to any conduct which another party did which occurred after the petition for election was filed with the NLRB.

If the employer before an election, promised a new benefit to employees or an improved benefit, or if he threatens the loss of an existing benefit, it may be grounds for filing objections. If the employer or union makes a statement to employees that seriously misrepresents the facts, it is also objectionable.

If objections are filed to the election or if the challenged ballots could affect the outcome, the NLRB agent usually conducts an investigation to determine the facts. He will ask the parties to provide witnesses to help him determine the facts. Sometimes in a close case or where he is unable to determine the facts because of conflicting versions of what happened, the regional director may schedule a hearing on objections or challenged ballots. This is a formal hearing at which a hearing officer, usually from the NLRB regional office, will participate, witnesses will be called to testify, and a court reporter will take down their testimony. It will be conducted somewhat like a court trial but it is less formal. If an individual files the petition in the matter, he may desire to be represented by an attorney, in which case the individual will be expected to make a complete record but he cannot interview witnesses for other parties before the hearing.

After the hearing closes the hearing officer will prepare a lengthy report finding facts and analyzing the law, with a recommendation. Copies will be served upon all parties to the proceeding. The decision of the hearing officer may be appealed either to the regional director or to the Board. The report will inform the parties of the procedure used to appeal.

Employees out on an economic strike (a strike seeking higher wages, better hours, or working conditions, and not caused or prolonged by a "serious" unfair labor practice by the employer) may vote in an election even though they are permanently replaced. Their replacements are also eligible to vote in the election. However, if the strike began more than 12 months before the date of the election, strikers are usually not eligible to vote.

Certification

If no objections are filed in the five-day period after balloting, and if challenged ballots could not change the outcome of the election, the NLRB regional office issues a document. It either certifies that the union is the bargaining representative, or certifies that the union lost.

If objections to the election are filed within the five days, the NLRB investigates them and if they are found to have merit it conducts another election. If challenged ballots could determine the outcome of the election, the NLRB investigates them and rules on whether the individuals were eligible to vote. If the NLRB finds them to be eligible it opens the challenge ballot envelope for each eligible employee, counts the ballots, and certifies whether the union won.

NLRB AND UNFAIR LABOR PRACTICES

Charge form An employee may file a charge with the NLRB against either an employer or a union, claiming that it engaged in an unfair labor practice. There is a six months' "statute of limitations" in the law, so that a charge may not be filed based upon an event which occurred more than six months earlier. The NLRB regional office will provide forms and help in preparing that form if requested. The "charge" form must be signed before it is filed. The NLRB will mail a copy to the employer and to the union. There is no fee by the NLRB to file a charge, even though it results in a lengthy trial and appeals. A "charge party" is not required to be represented by an attorney, but he may hire one and pay his usual fee. The charging party's attorney will assist the NLRB's attorney.

Rights of employees The heart of the National Labor Relations Act is Section 7, which states the rights of employees. Certain acts of an employer infringe upon those rights and constitute an employer unfair labor practice. Certain acts of a union or its agents infringe upon those rights of employees and constitute a union unfair labor practice. However, there are many possible acts of an employer or a union which are unfair, yet, do not constitute an unfair labor practice. Section 7 states as follows:

> Employees shall have the right to self-organization, to form, join, or assist labor organizations, to bargain collectively through representatives of their own choosing, and to engage in other concerted activities for the purpose of collective bargaining or other mutual aid or protection, and shall also have the right to refrain from any or all of such activities except to the extent that such right may be affected by an agreement requiring membership in a labor organization as a condition of employment as authorized in Section 8 (a) (3).

EMPLOYER UNFAIR LABOR PRACTICES

Section 8(a)(1) makes it an unfair labor practice for an employer "to interfere with, restrain, or coerce employees in the exercise of rights guaranteed in Section 7."

Interference, restraint, or coercion

If the employer has committed any unfair labor practice it automatically violates Section 8(a)(1). Other types of employer activity which would be an "independent" violation of Section 8(a)(1) are:

1. Questioning employees about their union activities or membership in circumstances that will tend to create fear by the employees;
2. Spying on union meetings;
3. Threatening employees with loss of jobs or benefits if they should join or vote for a union;
4. Granting wage increases timed to discourage employees from forming or voting for a union; or
5. Disciplining a group of employees for peacefully complaining about wages or working conditions even though there is no union involved.

Section 8(a)(2) makes it an unfair labor practice for an employer "to dominate or interfere with the formation or administration" of a union "or contribute financial or other support to it." An employer violates this section by:

Unlawful assistance to union

1. Taking an active part in organizing a committee or plan to represent employees in dealing with the employer regarding wages or working conditions;
2. Bringing pressure on employees to join a union except in the enforcement of a lawful union security agreement;
3. Permitting one of two or more unions which are competing to represent employees to solicit employees on company property during working hours but denying that privilege to other unions;

4. Recognizing, negotiating, or signing a contract with a union which does not represent a majority of his employees (except that in the construction industry it may not be unlawful); or

5. When buying an additional plant or store or similar business to agree to put those employees under an existing contract without proof that the union represents a majority of those employees.

Discrimination   Section 8(*a*)(3) makes it unlawful for an employer to refuse to hire, or to discharge or otherwise discriminate in employment terms or conditions against an employee because he is a member of a union. An employer cannot:

Fire an employee because he engaged in a lawful strike;

Close or sell a plant or a department because the employees there are organizing or have organized a union which the employer does not want to deal with;

Refuse to hire an employee because he is or is not a member of a particular union;

Fire an employee because he is not a member of the union when he has not been employed for 30 days (7 days in the construction industry); or

Subcontract out work because a union organizes the employees in that department.

An employer cannot fire employees who engage in a lawful strike, but he may "permanently replace" them. However, if the striker asks to return and the employer later has a job vacancy which the striker can satisfactorily do then the employer must give preference to the striker over a new job applicant.

An employer may terminate employees under the following circumstances: who strike over a grievance when there is a contract which has a "no strike" clause, or which provides for arbitration of that grievance; who strike in furtherance of an unfair labor practice by a union; who strike before the union gives to the employer and to a government mediator certain notices near the end of a contract; or who commit acts of violence during an otherwise lawful strike.

An employer may lay off or terminate for cause an employee even though he is a member of a union.

An employer may not terminate an employee because he is not a member of a union unless there is a contract with a lawful union security provision, the union requests the termination, and the employer believes that the reason for the union's request is that the employee has not offered to pay to the union the uniformly required initiation fee and the regular periodic dues. In a state with a "right to work law" the union cannot require that the employer fire any employee for failure to pay any fee to the union.

If the union has asked an employer to terminate an employee, and he has offered to the union the initiation fee and any monthly dues required since his employment under the current contract, he should inform the employer immediately. An employer, when faced with a request by a union to fire someone for not being a union member, should ask the employee for his version of the facts. If the employee has offered to the union the initiation fee and current dues, the employer should seek legal advice on what to do.

Section 8(*a*)(4) protects an employee who files **Protection of** an election petition or an unfair labor practice **witnesses** charge, or who testifies in an election or unfair labor practice matter before the NLRB. An employer may not refuse to promote, nor may an employer lay off or discharge or otherwise discipline an employee for using the processes of the NLRB during non-working time.

Refusal to bargain   Section 8(a)(5) requires that an employer bargain in good faith with the union which represents a majority of his employees. This duty to bargain applies in the negotiation of changes in an existing contract.

An employer has a duty upon request of the union to meet and confer with the union at reasonable times and places, in an attempt to reach an agreement. However, the employer cannot be compelled by the NLRB to agree to any particular term or condition of employment or wages which the employer has not himself agreed to.

Upon request of the union the employer must supply information "relevant and necessary" to allow the union to bargain intelligently and effectively. This information might include a list of the names, job classifications, wage rates, and date of hire or seniority date for all employees in the bargaining unit represented by the union.

If an agreement is reached on all subjects, upon request of the union, the employer must sign the contract which states their agreement.

The employer cannot make changes from existing wages, hours, terms, or conditions of employment without at least notifying the union of that change. However, if the employer in the past has taken particular action, such as subcontracting without notifying the union, then the employer may continue that past practice. Sometimes a union in a contract agrees that an employer may take particular action without consulting or notifying the union. An employer may also make changes in minor matters without consulting the union. An employer may not usually grant a wage increase without first consulting the union, unless the contract permits it or the employer is following his past practice of granting an increase to individual employees. However, if the employer and the union are negotiating for a contract and the employer has made an offer to the union of a stated amount of wage increase and the parties have reached an "impasse" in bargaining so that neither is willing to change its offer or proposal, then the employer may put into effect its last wage offer.

If there is a contract with a provision that disputes may be taken to arbitration, the NLRB may require the union to go to arbitration rather than to the NLRB.

An individual employee has the right to discuss with his foreman, supervisor, or anyone else in management any particular grievance or complaint and to "adjust" that complaint as long as the "adjustment" agreed to is not inconsistent with the terms of the collective bargaining contract. However, if the employee insists that the union agent be present in the discussion between the employee and the employer, the employer should agree. An individual employee may sign an individual contract of employment with the employer but the terms of that individual contract cannot conflict with the terms of a collective bargaining agreement which also covers him. If there is such conflict then the collective bargaining agreement controls.

If an employer buys part or all of the plant and equipment and maintains substantially the same suppliers and customers, and hires substantially the same employees of a predecessor employer, it may be a "successor employer." A successor employer usually has a duty to recognize and bargain with the union which represented the seller's employees. However, a successor is usually not bound by the seller's collective bargaining agreement.

Sometimes a group of employers bargain as a group with a union and have a practice of agreeing to the same terms and conditions of employment.

Those employers sometimes have a formal association. When they reach an agreement with the union on the terms of a contract it usually applies to all of the employers in that unit. Sometimes each employer signs a copy of the same document, or a spokesman for all of the employers in the unit signs. Such a group is called a "multiemployer bargaining unit." An employer may withdraw from such a bargaining unit if he gives clear notice to the union of his withdrawal at a proper time, before negotiations actually begin in that unit. The union may also withdraw from the unit by giving a "timely" notice to all the employers that it will bargain with them on a separate basis.

UNION UNFAIR LABOR PRACTICES

Restraint and coercion Section $8(b)(1)(A)$ makes it an unfair labor practice for a union to "restrain or coerce" employees in the exercise of the rights guaranteed in Section 7.

A union may adopt internal rules or bylaws governing its members, and enforce those rules or bylaws to a certain extent without violating the National Labor Relations Act. However, if those rules govern the conduct of a union member in his relation with his employer, then the union, by preparing or enforcing those rules, may restrain or coerce employees in violation of Section $8(b)(1)(A)$. For example, a union may lawfully fine a member for working during a lawful strike or for not attending a regular union meeting. A union may also terminate the membership of, but not fine, a member who files an NLRB petition to decertify the union. If an employee joined the union only because he is covered by a contract with a union security clause (such as a 30-day or 8-day union shop clause), then the union has less freedom to discipline the member.

Members may be required to first follow the

procedure provided in the union's constitution and bylaws, such as filing a charge within the union, so long as that procedure does not require more than four months' time, before the NLRB will rule that the union's conduct violated the National Labor Relations Act. However, the statute of limitations for the National Labor Relations Act is only six months, so a charge should be filed with the NLRB within that time period.

If union members send to the union a notice of their resignation, they may then engage in conduct, such as going through a picket line to work, and if the union then attempts to discipline them such as by a fine, the union may violate Section 8(b)(1)(A). The members may not be required to follow the complete procedure provided in the union constitution or bylaws for resigning from union membership, if that procedure is too lengthy and members are not clearly informed of the procedure. The member should send a signed letter (keeping a copy for himself) by registered mail or certified mail, return receipt requested, to the union. The letter should clearly state that the member is resigning his membership, and it should be signed by the member, stating his address and book or union member number. The union cannot later attempt to get the employer to fire him under the terms of a "union security" agreement, so long as he offers to pay to the union an amount equal to the union's initiation fee and each month's current dues.

A union which is the exclusive bargaining representative of employees owes to them a duty to represent them fairly whether or not they are a member of the union, and regardless of their race, color, or sex.

Other activities by a union or its agent (such as a business agent, and usually a steward or individuals picketing) which violate Section 8(b)(1)(A) include:

1. Mass-picketing which prevents employees or others from going into or out of the employer's premises,
2. Acts of violence on the picket line,
3. Threatening to injure nonstriking employees,
4. Threatening employees that they will lose their job if they are not a member of the union in good standing (but if there is a valid contract in effect with a union shop clause such statement may not be an unlawful threat),
5. Entering into a contract with an employer when the union has not been chosen by a majority of the employees in that bargaining unit,
6. Maintaining a seniority arrangement with an employer which is discriminatory, because it favors union members or individuals of a particular race, color, or sex, and
7. Refusing to register or refer an individual in the union-operated exclusive hiring hall because he is not a member in good standing with the union.

Restraint and coercion of employer representatives

Section 8(b)(1)(B) makes it unlawful for a union "to restrain or coerce an employer in the selection of his representatives for the purposes of collective bargaining or the adjustment of grievances."

A union cannot insist that an employer not have a particular individual, such as a supervisor, labor consultant, or attorney, represent the employer in contract negotiations or in handling grievances. A union cannot threaten to discipline a member because of acts he did for the employer while acting as a supervisor for the employer. A union cannot strike one or more members of a multiemployer association with an object to get them to sign individual contracts and break away from the association.

Section 8(*b*)(2) makes it an unfair labor practice for a union "to cause or attempt to cause an
employer to discriminate against an employee in
violation of subsection (*a*)(3). . . ."

A union violates Section 8(*b*)(2) by requesting
that an employer discharge an employee because
he is not a member of that union, or not a member
in "good standing" unless there is a lawful "union
security" agreement. A "closed shop," requiring that
an employee be a member of the union before he
can be hired, is made unlawful. Any union security
agreement must permit the employee a 30-day "grace
period" before he can be required to make any payment to the union. However, in the construction industry he can be required to make such payment
after 7 days.

An employee cannot be discharged because he is
not a member of the union so long as he has offered to pay any initiation fee uniformly required
and the periodic dues, such as monthly dues. This
offer should be in the form of cash or money order,
although a personal check is usually considered to
be sufficient. An employee cannot lawfully be discharged if he offers to pay such initiation fees and
the current month's dues plus any other dues which
began during the current collective bargaining agreement, or from the period 30 days after the employee
was hired (7 days in construction), whichever is
later. An employee cannot be required to sign an
application for membership in the union or to take
an oath of allegiance to the union or to its constitution and bylaws. An employee also cannot be required to pay a fine or an assessment, so long as he
pays or offers to pay the initiation fees uniformly
required and the periodic dues. However, the union
can attempt to collect a fine or assessment from a
member of the union by internal union procedures,

and in some states it may then go into court to seek payment of that fine or assessment. The union cannot insist that the employer fire the employee because he has not paid such fine or assessment.

Approximately 20 states have passed a "right to work law." These prohibit agreements between an employer and a union which require payment of dues or fees to a union or membership in a union. The National Labor Relations Act as amended permits these state laws. If an employee who lives in a state with such a "right to work law" chooses not to make any payment of initiation fees or dues to the union, it cannot request that the employer fire the employee, and any provision in a collective bargaining agreement requiring membership or payment of fees to the unions would be invalid and not enforceable. However, an employee may join a union if he wishes.

Hiring halls   If an employer and a union have an agreement or practice that if the employer hires anyone he must first give a hiring hall operated by the union the opportunity to refer or dispatch any applicant, it is usually lawful unless the dispatcher, in making referrals, favors union members over others. The union may charge referral fees if the amount of the fee is reasonably related to the cost of operating the hiring hall. The union may also give preference to "local people" in referrals, at least in the construction industry. If the dispatcher discriminates in referrals against individuals who are not members in good standing of the local, the union violates this section and is liable for any back pay lost because of this discriminatory practice.

If the dispatcher refuses to let an individual register with an "exclusive" hiring hall, and the individual believes that he is qualified to perform the work, he should inquire about the procedure for testing applicants. If there is an employee-union committee the individual should present evidence of training or experience (such as paycheck stubs, letters from employers, or military officers) to the committee or the dispatcher. Keep a photocopy of any documents provided. Look for any document on the bulletin board stating rules for the hiring hall and the appeal procedure. An individual should follow that appeal procedure if he believes he was wrongfully denied the right to register. If he does not get a satisfactory answer within a few days, the individual should visit, phone, or write the NLRB regional office and ask to file an unfair labor practice charge. A job applicant is not required to first follow any procedures set out in the collective bargaining agreement or in the hiring hall rules before filing a charge of discrimination against the union. However, after filing a charge, the NLRB may require him to follow that procedure.

If the agreement or practice of the employer permits him to hire from other sources without requiring that job applicants be referred to him by the union hiring hall, the union may in referrals give preference to its members.

Section 8(*b*)(3) makes it unlawful for a union which represents the employees to refuse to bargain collectively in good faith with the employer. **Refusal to bargain**

A union cannot strike at the end of a contract or during the "automatic renewal period" unless it first gives to the employer a 60-day notice to negotiate changes required by Section 8(*d*) of the National Labor Relations Act, a 30-day notice to the Federal Mediation and Conciliation Service, and a 30-day notice to a state mediator (if that state has a state mediator). The union must also give the other notices (usually 60 to 90 days) required in the collective bargaining agreement. The union must wait

until the end of all those time periods before striking. Any employee who strikes before the end of
that "cooling-off period" may be fired by the employer.

A union which is the exclusive representative of
employees has a duty to meet at reasonable times
with the employer or his representative and confer
in good faith on wages, hours, or other terms or
conditions of employment, and if an agreement is
reached in negotiations the union must upon request
sign a copy of that agreement. A union does not bargain in good faith if it insists that the employer sign
its "standard" or "pattern" contract, without con-
cessions or modifications.

The union has a duty to represent fairly all of the
employees in the bargaining unit whether they are
members of the union or not. A union cannot discriminate against those employees for irrelevant or
arbitrary reasons, such as to discriminate against
a group of employees because of their race, color,
or sex.

Neither a union nor an employer can insist upon
"nonmandatory" subjects of bargaining in negotiations. For example, the union cannot insist that the
contract cover employees who are outside the bargaining unit certified by the NLRB. It cannot strike
or harass an employer, who is a member of a multiemployer bargaining unit, to force that employer to
sign a separate contract with the union or to withdraw from the multiemployer unit. The union cannot in negotiations insist that the employer settle a
pending grievance other than by taking it to arbitration. The union cannot insist upon an unlawful
cause, such as a "hot cargo" agreement or a "closed
shop" agreement, or any other form of union security which is unlawful in that state. The union cannot insist that supervisors who handle grievances for
the employer become union members.

Section 8(e) of the National Labor Relations Act makes it unlawful for an employer or a union to enter into a "hot cargo" agreement. This is an agreement, written or verbal, in which the employer stops or agrees to stop doing business with another employer. In the construction industry such a "hot cargo" agreement is lawful when limited to the contracting or subcontracting of work to be done at the job site, and the union can enforce it by arbitration or a court action but cannot picket or threaten to picket to enforce it. In the garment industry a "hot cargo" agreement may not be unlawful.

Hot cargo

Section 8(b)(4)(A) makes it unlawful for a union to request or "induce or encourage" an individual employee not to work, not to handle goods, or to "threaten, coerce, or restrain" an employer or other "person" to force any employer or independent contractor to enter into a "hot cargo" agreement.

Section 8(b)(4)(A) also prohibits such conduct by a union to force or require any employer or independent contractor to join any union, or to join any employer organization.

Forcing independent contractors

It is often difficult to determine whether an individual is an independent contractor or is an employee. In general, if an individual furnishes his own expensive machinery such as a truck or a tractor, if he has considerable right to determine his hours and days of work and the details as to how he does that work, if he does similar work for other employers, and advertises his business, then he is probably an independent contractor, not an employee.

Section 8(b)(4)(B) makes it unlawful for a union to "induce or encourage" an individual not to work or not to handle goods, or to "threaten, coerce, or restrain" an employer or other "person," where the object is to cause that person not to use or handle

Secondary boycotts

the products of anyone else or to stop doing business with him. This section also prohibits similar conduct where the object is to require any other employer to bargain with or sign a contract with a union, unless that union has been certified by the NLRB as the representative of those employees.

In general, if a union has a labor dispute with one person or employer (the "primary employer"), it must take steps to limit the effect of its action against that "primary" on neutrals or "secondary employers." For example, if a union has a dispute with a subcontractor who is working at a jobsite where a general contractor and other persons are employed, the union may picket the subcontractor with whom it has the dispute at that jobsite provided that (1) the picket signs make it clear that the only dispute is with the subcontractor and not with any other person, (2) its picketing is limited to times when the subcontractor's employees are present at the site, (3) its picketing is limited to places close to the operation of the subcontractor's employees, and (4) the subcontractor's employees are engaged in his normal subcontracting work at those premises. If a separate gate is established only for that subcontractor and his employees or deliveries, then the union can picket only at that gate and not at gates used by others.

It may not be unlawful for a union to picket or threaten to picket another employer who is an "ally" of the primary employer. If the primary and secondary employers are commonly owned and controlled or have "closely integrated operations" they may be allies. Likewise, if the secondary employer does "struck work" which would normally be done by the primary, they may be allies.

Coercion to force recognition   Section $8(b)(4)(C)$ makes it unlawful for a union to induce or encourage an individual employee not

to work or not to handle goods, or to threaten, coerce, or restrain an employer or other person, where
the union has an object to force or require any employer to bargain with or sign a contract with any
union. However, if that union has been certified by
the NLRB as the bargaining representative it may
be lawful.

Section 8(b)(4)(D) makes it unlawful for a union
to induce or encourage an individual employee not
to work or not to handle goods, or to threaten, coerce, or restrain an employer or other person, with
an object to force or require any employer to assign
particular work to a group of employees. However,
if that employer is failing to conform to an order of
the NLRB or certification of the NLRB, it is not unlawful. For example, if a union representing ironworkers threatens to picket if it is not assigned the
work of installing metal roofing then the ironworkers' union may violate this section of the law. However, if the ironworkers' union had won an NLRB
election among employees of that employer, or if
the NLRB had issued an order awarding this kind
of work done by that employer to employees represented by the ironworkers' union, then such threat
may not be unlawful.

Jurisdictional disputes

Section 10(k) of the law provides that if there is
such a threat of a work stoppage by a union seeking
particular work then the NLRB may schedule a hearing, and upon the basis of evidence presented, the
NLRB will make an assignment of the work in dispute to a particular "trade, craft, or class." In the
hearing the NLRB will want testimony and documents showing the skills and work involved; any
certifications of the union(s) by the NLRB, the past
practice by the employer and in the industry; any
agreement between union(s) and between the employers and the union; awards of arbitrators, joint

boards or parent unions in the same or related cases; the assignment of work made by the employer; and the efficient operation of the employer's business.

Excessive or discriminatory membership fees

Section 8(b)(5) makes it unlawful for a union which has a "union security agreement" with an employer to charge a fee "which the Board finds excessive or discriminatory under the circumstances." If the employer, for example, has a collective bargaining agreement with a union which provides that after 30 days employees must become a member of the union, then it is unlawful for the union to charge an excessive initiation fee or dues.

The practices and customs of other labor organizations in that industry and the wages paid to the employees will be considered in determining whether the fees are excessive. If a fee is imposed not to provide needed additional revenues for the local union but to maintain in effect a closed shop by a fee so high that it discourages entrance into the industry, then it violates this section. A reinstatement fee for old members slightly higher than the initiation fee for new members may be lawful under this section.

Featherbedding

Section 8(b)(6) makes it unlawful for a union "to cause or attempt to cause an employer to pay or deliver or agree to pay or deliver any money or other thing of value in the nature of exaction, for services which are not performed or not to be performed." This section does not prohibit payments such as employees' wages during lunch, rest, waiting, or vacation periods, or for reporting for duty to determine whether work is to be done.

Picketing for organization, recognition, or bargaining

Section 8(b)(7) makes it unlawful for a union, unless it is "currently certified" as the representative of the employees, to picket or threaten to picket an employer to force the employer to bargain with the union or to sign a contract with it where (*a*) the employer has lawfully recognized a different union, *or* (*b*) within the last 12 months a "valid" election has been conducted by the NLRB, *or* (*c*) the picketing continues for more than a reasonable period of time, not more than 30 days, without the filing of a petition for an election.

Sometimes a union claims that its picketing is only to inform the public that the employer does not employ members of the union or have a contract with it. This picketing may be lawful unless "an effect" of the picketing is to induce individuals not to perform services or to make deliveries or pick up goods.

Unions sometimes claim that their picketing is only to inform the public that the employer does not pay "standard" wages or other benefits. This picketing may be lawful unless it is shown that an object of the picketing is to get employees to join the union or to cause the employer to bargain with or sign a contract with the union.

If a charge is filed claiming that picketing is in violation of Section 8(*b*)(7)(*C*) then the employer or an individual (such as an employee) may file a petition for an "expedited" election. If the NLRB regional director finds that the picketing apparently has such a purpose, he may order the election.

Injunctions

If the regional director of the NLRB believes that there is merit to a charge that the union violated Section 8(*b*)(4) or Section 8(*b*)(7) and there is current picketing or a work stoppage or the threat of one, he will seek an injunction against the unlawful acts in a federal district court. If the injunction is granted it normally is in effect until the matter is ultimately decided by the Board on its merits.

The regional director may, under another section of the law, seek an injunction against unfair labor practices of either an employer or a union, but this kind of injunction is not common.

Unfair labor practice procedure

If the regional director of the NLRB believes that an employer or a union has committed an unfair labor practice as charged he will first give that party an opportunity to settle the matter. This consists, as a minimum, of the signing of a standard "informal" settlement agreement plus the signing and posting of a "notice" on its bulletin board for at least 60 days. A "formal" settlement agreement consists of a document signed by the parties stating the background facts about the employer or the union, the conduct which is believed to be an unfair labor practice, and an agreement to the entry of an order of the NLRB in a particular form.

If there is no satisfactory signed settlement agreement, the regional director will issue a complaint and schedule a hearing before an NLRB administrative law judge. The charged party (respondent) has at least 10 days to file a written answer to the complaint. Failure to answer each claim made in the complaint will be treated as an admission that the claim is true.

The hearing before the judge is usually scheduled about two months after the complaint issues, in the city where the respondent is located or where most of the conduct claimed to be unlawful occurred. The hearing before the judge is formal, similar to a court trial without a jury. The rules of procedure of the federal district courts are followed. A court reporter takes down testimony. The attorney for the NLRB regional director acts as prosecutor, calling witnesses, each of whom is subject to cross-examination. The charging party may also be represented by an attorney, but it is not necessary, since the attorney for the regional director represents the public and the charging party. The respondent is usually represented by an attorney. After the NLRB attorney "closes" his case, the respondent may call witnesses and present testimony. A closing argument may be made and briefs may be filed with the judge.

About two months or more after the trial is completed, the judge prepares a written decision, copies of which are served upon the parties, finding in detail the facts, resolving credibility (deciding who is correct, where there is a dispute as to what happened), and interpreting the law to issue a written decision. Within 20 days, any party may file an appeal (take exceptions) to his decision. The exceptions must state exactly what page and line of the judge's decision is believed to be wrong. A brief, arguing the "facts" and the law from NLRB or court cases, may also be prepared. A copy of the exceptions and brief must be served upon each of the other parties.

A few months later the National Labor Relations Board in Washington, D.C. will issue an order adopting, modifying, or reversing the judge's decision. The decision of the Board may be appealed to a U.S. Circuit Court of Appeals. If the Board finds an unlawful practice and the respondent does not comply with the Board's order, the Board may file a petition for enforcement of its order with the U.S. Circuit Court of Appeals. The decision of the Court may be appealed to the U.S. Supreme Court.

Remedies

The Board's order attempts to remedy any unfair labor practice found. However, the Board does not have authority to punish the respondent, or to force it to admit that it violated the act. The usual language for the Board's notices is "we will not . . . ." The respondent is thus required to agree that it will not engage in certain unlawful acts but it is not required to admit that it has in the past engaged in such acts.

If an employer is found to have unlawfully assisted a union it is required to agree that it will not unlawfully assist the named union. If the employer is found to have unlawfully dominated a union it will be asked to "disestablish" that union. If it is found to have unlawfully discharged an employee because of his union activity, the employer will be asked to reinstate the employee and to pay back pay, plus interest at 6 percent. If the Board finds that an employer has not bargained in good faith with the union it will be asked to sign the notice stating that it will bargain in good faith.

If a union is found to have unlawfully caused the employer to discharge an employee for some reason, other than his failure to pay or offer to pay the uniform initiation fee or periodic dues, then the union will be asked to pay back pay plus interest at 6 percent. The union will also be asked to notify the employer in writing that it has no objections to his taking back the named individual. If the union is found to have charged unlawful fees, such as dues before 30 days of employment, assessments, or excessive or discriminatory fees, then the union will be ordered to refund to employees the unlawful part of any fees paid. If the union is found to have engaged in picketing or other conduct in violation of the law, it will be ordered to "cease and desist" from such unlawful conduct.

Sometimes an unfair labor practice charge is filed against both an employer and the union and both are found to have committed the unlawful act as charged. The employer and the union are each "jointly and severally" liable. Thus, either the employer or the union could be ordered to pay the complete amount of any money owed.

If the Board finds that the employer unlawfully discharged or refused to take back a striker, the Board will not order that he be paid back pay from the date earlier than the time when he makes an "unconditional" offer to return to work. However, this offer could be made by the union or another employee on that employee's behalf.

If an individual is eligible for back pay because of an unlawful act by an employer or a union or both, he has a duty to look for other similar work in his area. He should register with the state employment office and look for work elsewhere. The Board will deduct earnings from "interim employment" since his discharge, but he may claim credit for expenses of looking for other work. He should keep a record of such expenses. The individual must notify the NLRB agent assigned to the case of his change of address.

STRIKES AND PICKETING

The constitution of most local and international unions requires a vote on the employer's last offer before employees strike for a contract seeking better wages, hours, or working conditions. To authorize a strike, many unions require a vote of a majority of two thirds of those members present in a meeting or of members voting by mail ballots. Some unions permit a final contract offer by the employer to be accepted by a majority vote but require a two-thirds vote to authorize a strike. A strike can usually be ended by a majority vote. A secret ballot or paper ballot is sometimes required.

Authorizing strikes

International unions often require that a local union follow the procedure in the international's constitution before it will pay benefits to employees out on strike. Only members in good standing can receive strike benefits from most unions, and benefits are usually not paid for the first week of a strike. Many unions do not pay strike benefits to a member who works during part of the strike, then quits work to join the strikers. Even if members of a local union vote to strike, the international union may assign an international representative to investigate, and it may decide not to pay strike benefits if it believes there is little chance of "winning" the strike, if the local union's position in negotiations is not fair, or if there is little money in the strike fund. Benefits are usually paid for a lockout under the same terms as strike benefits.

The National Labor Relations Board does not require a vote on an employer's offer before the union rejects it. (An exception is that for threatened or actual strikes or lockouts which cause a "national emergency," the NLRB may conduct a secret ballot election among employees on whether to accept the employer's last offer.) The NLRB also does not require a vote before a strike is called. If there is a vote on an employer's offer or on whether to authorize a strike, the NLRB does not require that it be by secret ballot or by a majority vote. The NLRB does not require that employees who are not members in good standing be permitted to vote. The NLRB does not prohibit voting by members not employed by the particular employer involved. In general, the NLRB refuses to get involved in these matters, on the theory that they deal with relations between the union and the employees, not "wages, hours, and other terms and conditions of work" of employees.

If the union does not conduct a secret ballot vote on an employer's last offer, or on whether to strike, and the union's action (or failure to act) is contrary to the union's constitution and bylaws, then a member can sue the union and its officers in court. Most courts hold that a union's constitution and bylaws are a "contract" between the union and its members, and can be enforced in court, by an injunction or a lawsuit for money damages, just like any other contract.

A "strike" is the refusal to perform work, usually by a group of two or more employees. Sometimes in a strike there is no picketing. It is common in the construction industry for one craft to go on strike for a new contract without posting any pickets at jobs, since picketing might cause other crafts to lose work.

An "economic" strike is one in which employees as a group quit work to support their union's efforts to get better wages, hours, or working conditions from their employer. To be lawful the union must first give the proper notices required under the National Labor Relations Act, as amended — if there is an agreement, 60 days' notice to the employer and 30 days' notice to the Federal Mediation and Conciliation Service and to the state mediation agency (if the state has a mediator). The union must also give the employer any other notice required by the collective bargaining agreement. The union must wait until the 60 and 30 days have expired, as well as any time period required by the collective bargaining agreement, before striking. If the employees strike before all of these time periods have expired, the employer can terminate them even though he hasn't hired "permanent replacements" to fill their jobs, and the employer can sue the union for money damages.

If a striker is "permanently replaced" he is no longer an employee. However, if the employer later has a vacancy in a job which he can do, the employer must give him preference over a "new hire," if the striker lets the employer know he wants to return to work and he is readily available when needed.

If in the contract there is either a "no strike clause" or a provision that a grievance may be filed over a particular dispute and it can be taken to arbitration which would be binding upon the employer, then employees cannot strike over such a "gripe" or grievance. If employees strike they may be terminated even though the employer hasn't hired permanent replacements, and the employer can seek a court injunction against the strike and money damages from the union.

However, if employees go on strike protesting a "serious" unfair labor practice of the employer, and the employer terminates them, the NLRB may order the employees reinstated. But, even if an employee goes on strike to protest an employer's unfair labor practice, and there is a contract with a "no strike clause" applying to him, the NLRB will not order the employer to reinstate the individual unless the NLRB finds that unfair labor practice is "serious."

If particular employees are proven to have done acts of violence, such as mass picketing or making serious threats during a strike, the NLRB will not order the employer to take them back even though the strike itself is lawful.

Sometimes an employer will "lock out" employees in a labor dispute. If he has grounds for believing the union will probably strike, the employer may usually lawfully lock out employees. The employer must meet the requirements of the contract — if it has a "no strike, no lock out" clause he may not lock out employees while the contract is in effect. If a group of employees are on strike and another group of employees, not on strike, cannot work full-time efficiently because their work is dependent upon the strikers, the employer may lay off employees not in the group represented by the union.

If a union strikes some employers who are members of an association but not other members (a "whipsaw" strike), the employers who are not struck may lay off their employees "to preserve the bargaining unit," yet continue to operate with temporary hires. The employers who are struck may replace the strikers with "permanent" employees.

Sometimes a union or individuals will picket an employer or some other location even though there is no strike. "Picketing" is usually considered to be patrolling with a placard or wearing an apron with a message printed on it. Sometimes picketing does not involve patrolling, but only the placing of a sign on a parked car or on posts stuck into the ground. "Handbilling" is the passing out of handbills, usually to the public, with a message printed on them. Someimes it is difficult to distinguish between picketing and handbilling, especially if copies of the handbill are fastened to a nearby post, building, or other object.

If a union represents the employees at a place being picketed, it usually has "on strike" printed in large letters on the picket signs or aprons. If the strike is lawful (after the proper notices have been given and if the strike is not in violation of a collective bargaining agreement), the pickets and other union agents may lawfully attempt to persuade everyone not to go through the picket line. However, the union cannot use or threaten to use violence, or use large groups of pickets to block entrances and exits.

As a general rule, picketing must be limited to the business location of the employer whose employees are on strike (the "struck employer"). If the struck employer shares a business location with another employer, or if the struck employer is having a contractor do work on his premises, and he sets up and clearly marks a gate set aside for that contractor and his employees and deliveries, then the striking union cannot lawfully picket at that "separate gate." To do so would be a "secondary boycott." [See the discussion of Union Labor Practices, Section 8(b)(4)(B), at page 35.] However, if the contractor is doing some work which would normally be done by employees on strike, the union may picket even at the separate gate. As a general rule, pickets cannot picket on private property, but under some circumstances they may picket on a parking lot of a large shopping center.

Sometimes a union pickets an employer to persuade the employees to join the union, or to force the employer to recognize the union as the representative of his employees, and to negotiate or sign a contract with the union. The union usually tries to get employees to sign cards authorizing the union to represent them, or cards applying for membership in the union. The National Labor Relations Act, as amended, limits this kind of picketing to 30 days, unless the union is successful in getting a majority of the employees to support the union, or unless a petition for an NLRB election is filed. [See the discussion of Union Unfair Labor Practices, Section 8(b)(7), at page 38.]

Unions sometimes do "informational" or "advertising" or "free speech" picketing to inform the public that the employer being picketed does not employ members of the union, or have a contract with the union. This picketing may be lawful if it is truthful and the union does not ask customers or employees or others (such as deliverymen) not to cross the picket line. If the union's picketing has an effect to cause a stoppage of deliveries or pickups, or to cause employees not to work, it may be limited to 30 days, by Section 8(b)(7)(C) of the National Labor Relations Act.

Another type of picketing is "union standards picketing," with signs claiming that the employer is "unfair" and that his employees do not receive the "area standards" wage rate, fringe benefits, and working conditions. If the union has actual knowledge that the employees' wages, fringe benefits, and working conditions are not as good as those in the area, this picketing may be lawful if conducted at the proper times and places. However, if the union pickets to cause the employer to pay the same wages and fringe benefits as provided in union contracts, the picketing may actually be to get the employer to bargain with the union, and may be limited to 30 days or less. [See the National Labor Relations Act, as amended, Section 8(*b*)(7)(*C*), as described above.]

A union may picket with signs stating that the employer "has committed unfair labor practices." If the union has filed an unfair labor practice charge with the NLRB against the employer, this may be a "free speech" type of picketing. But if the union does not represent a majority of the employees, and if it has tried to organize them, or has tried to get the employer to sign a contract, the purpose of this kind of picketing may be limited by the NLRB, as explained above. This is especially so if the NLRB dismissed the union's unfair labor practice charge after a finding that the charge did not have merit.

If an employer is faced with picketing which he believes is to organize his employees, he should ask the pickets and union agents what he can do to get rid of the pickets. If the union wants him to sign a contract he should ask for a copy of the contract to examine. The employer, his supervisors, and his employees could write notes showing names, dates, and time when an incident occurs (1) where pickets ask a truck driver not to cross the picket line, (2) where pickets or union agents ask employees not to cross to perform services, or (3) where pickets ask employees to sign union authorization cards.

The National Labor Relations Act, as amended, administered by the NLRB, gives employees the right to engage in a strike if they want to, if it is a lawful strike as outlined above.

Working during a strike or picketing

However, if an employee decides not to go through a picket line to work, either at his employer's premises or at the premises of another employer, he can usually be "permanently replaced." If there is a contract covering the employee and the contract has a no strike clause, or an agreement to take disputes to arbitration, an employee who refuses to cross to do his normal work can usually be terminated, as pointed out above, even though a replacement is not hired for his job. But, if the contract has a provision permitting an employee to refuse to cross a picket line "recognized" by his union or authorized in a particular way, then an employee may refuse to cross a picket line if it is recognized by his union or authorized in the manner spelled out in the contract.

If the union engages in picketing with large numbers of pickets and attempts to block entrances and exits to the employer's plant or premises, or if it adopts threats made by pickets to anyone who crosses picket lines, the employer being picketed could call the police to preserve law and order, and could go to a state court to get an injunction against the violence and blocking of entrances and exits. The employer or any individual could also go to the NLRB to file unfair labor practice charges against the union, for restraint and coercion of employees, a violation of Section 8(b)(1)(A) of the National Labor Relations Act, as amended.

If an employee misses work because of a strike, the NLRB will not order his employer to give him back pay for the time he was out, even though he was on strike to protest "serious" unfair labor practices by the employer. However, if it is an unfair labor practice strike and either the employee or his union makes a clear offer to the employer for the employee to return to work, then the employer may be required to pay back pay. The offer to return to work must not be qualified by some condition such as the employer's agreeing to the union's demands in negotiations or to take back some strikers whom he has no duty to take back. The employer would be allowed several days to take an employee back. If the employer can show that he doesn't have work available that an employee is qualified to do, then he may not be required to give back pay. However, if the strike is to protest the employer's unfair labor practices, he may be required to discharge replacements to create openings for strikers who want to return.

If an employee, who is a union member, works during a strike or if he crosses an "authorized" picket line, many unions provide that he may be disciplined. This usually means that any union member can file charges against him; a hearing would probably be held by the trial board of his local union, and he could be fined several hundred dollars or his membership in the union could be terminated. If the union fines a member, it may sue him in a state court to collect the fine, at least if the union constitution states that the union can sue in court to collect a fine. If it is a lawful strike, the NLRB probably won't help him if he voluntarily became a member of the union, even if the amount of the fine is unreasonable. If the strike is not lawful and a union officer threatens to fine a member or to schedule a trial because he worked, he could ask the NLRB to prepare a charge against the union for restraint and coercion; this is a violation of Section 8(b)(1)(A) of the National Labor Relations Act, as amended.

It is common practice by some unions, when labor negotiations are not making satisfactory progress, to prepare for a strike. One of the methods used by unions to cause employees to refuse to work during a strike is to attempt to get all employees to join the union. Some unions reduce or eliminate the usual initiation fee for a short period of time to entice them to become members. Once an employee is a member he may be afraid to work during the strike because of the possibility that the union may fine him for working.

If an employee wants to go through a picket line to perform work and the union picketing does not represent him, the employee could ask the picketing captain to give him a pass to go through. If the employee convinces the picket captain that he will not be doing work which is normally done by employees out on strike, the picket captain will probably give the employee a pass or refer him to the business agent of his union. If an employee does not get a pass he could phone his boss and explain the situation to him and ask what to do. If the employer wants the employee to come through the picket line but they are not sure what to do, either could phone the business agent of the union, explain the situation to him, and ask what to do. Some employers, such as public utilities, may have a legal duty to cross a picket line to perform services — those employers should use supervisors to perform the services if necessary.

If a union threatens to fine or to file charges against employees for crossing a picket line at the premises of any employer except their own employer, the employee should try to get a ruling by his business agent that the picketing was only "informational," "advertising," or "union standards." The employee should also ask his union agent if the picketing was authorized by and is recognized by the Central Labor Council or Building Trades Council, or by the member's union. If a member believes that the employees acted properly by crossing the picket line but the union still threatens to fine or discipline the employees, they should notify their supervisor. The supervisor should notify a supervisor or manager of the employer who was picketed. The member's statement may permit the picketed employer to prove that the union picketing his business is not just doing "advertising" or "free speech" picketing, but that it is doing more, such as trying to get recognition or to cause a secondary boycott.

If the constitution and bylaws of a union does not provide for a fine or other discipline of a member for working during a strike, or if the procedure stated in the constitution and bylaws is not followed, but the union disciplines an employee, he may sue the union in a federal or state court. (See the discussion "Controls over Internal Union Affairs," at page 58.)

If there is a lawful contract applying to employees which requires that an employee join the union after 30 days (or after 7 days in the construction industry), each employee should offer to pay to the union the current regular dues and initiation fee. If the union then levies a fine against an employee for working during a strike or picketing and attempts to get the employer to terminate him because he is not a "member in good standing," the employee should tell his employer. The employer should ask the employee to explain his version of what he and the union did. The employer should then ask the union agent for his version of the facts. If the employer finds that the employee has offered to pay dues and initiation fee he should not terminate the employee. If the employer wrongfully terminates the employee, he could go to the NLRB and file unfair labor practice charges against the union or the employer, or both.

If an employee is a member of a union, anticipates that there will be a strike, and wants to continue to work, he may resign or terminate his membership in the union. The union cannot then fine him for working during the strike. The employee should first ask the union for a withdrawal card. However, many unions will not give a withdrawal card shortly before or during a strike. If there is a procedure stated in the union constitution and bylaws for resigning his union membership, the employee should attempt to follow that procedure. If there is no stated procedure, he should write a letter to the union, keeping a carbon copy, stating that he is resigning or terminating his membership, effective immediately, and send it to the union by registered or certified mail, return receipt requested. If the employee believes that the union will refuse to accept the letter, also send a letter by regular mail. If an employee resigns from union membership after the strike has begun, some courts or the NLRB may hold that the union can fine him, at least for the time that he worked before his resignation letter was received by the union.

If an employee has resigned from union membership and the employer later signs a contract with the union having a "union security clause" requiring "membership" in the union, the employee does not have to become a "full member" of the union to hold his job. He can be required to offer to pay to the union an amount equal to the usual initiation fee or reinstatement fee, plus regular dues, usually each month. If an employee has terminated his membership to work during a strike, the union may properly refuse to permit him to become a "member in good standing."

"Membership" in a union, which may be required by the National Labor Relations Act, as amended, and a contract only requires offering to pay to the union an amount equal to the usual initiation or reinstatement fee, and regular dues. The union cannot cause an employee to lose employment because he hasn't taken an oath of allegiance to the union or its constitution and bylaws, or because he hasn't paid a fine or assessment. Some provisions in union constitutions are either unlawful, or are applied by union officers in situations so that they are unlawful under the National Labor Relations Act, as amended, or under other laws. If an employee did not voluntarily join the union, but only because he believed he had to join to keep his job due to a contract's union security clause, and the union threatens to have him fired if he works during a strike, he may contact the NLRB and ask it to prepare an unfair labor practice charge for the employee to file against the union.

If an individual lives in one of the 19 or more states (mostly in the South or Southwest) with a "right to work law" and the union attempts to get an employer to terminate an employee for not paying any fee, dues, fine, or assessment to the union, the employee may notify the NLRB and ask to file an unfair labor practice charge.

Paid by the union. Some unions pay a stated amount of money or food each week to employees on strike. The strike must first be authorized or approved by procedures set up in the union's constitution and bylaws. This usually means that a meeting of the members must be held, and a majority or more of those voting must approve the strike. An employee may be required to be a member of the union before he gets any benefits, and he may be required to do a certain amount of picket duty before being paid. An employee may be required to report any strike benefits received to the Internal Revenue Service and to pay taxes on it, particularly if the payments are not a "gift" but he is expected to do some picketing or other services to receive the payments.

Unemployment compensation. An employee cannot usually receive state employment benefits if he is not working because of a strike of employees in the same "bargaining unit" in which he is employed.

Benefits during a strike

Some states may allow unemployment compensation if an employee can show that the strike had little effect on the employer's production — that there was little "stoppage of work." An employee may be entitled to benefits if he can show that he received no benefit from the strike, such as picketing or a strike by a union which does not represent him, but which results in his being laid off for lack of work.

If an employee believes he is entitled to benefits he may apply at the local state employment office. If benefits are denied he may appeal by completing a simple form provided by the employment office. A hearing will be scheduled, usually at the same office a few weeks later. A written decision will be issued later. An employee may represent himself at the hearing, or a union agent or attorney may represent him. Likewise, an employer may represent himself or he may employ an attorney.

In some states, the employers pay all of the cost of unemployment benefits, and in all states they pay a large portion of the cost. One can understand why employers do not like to pay unemployment benefits if employees are on strike against an employer.

Welfare. If an individual can show that he has few assets and his debts are piling up, he can go to his local welfare office and apply for help. He may be entitled to buy food stamps which will permit him to buy a lot of food for a small cost. He may be entitled to payments of money, particularly if children are dependent upon his support.

DEMOCRACY IN UNIONS

In nearly every local union there is a small portion of the membership that attends meetings and holds offices in the union. From the point of view of those individuals, they are the dedicated members who do most of the work, often working many hours each week for little or no pay. From the point of view of other members, they are the "clique" which runs the union for their own benefit.

Employers often prefer to deal with union agents who have authority to make binding agreements, rather than truly "democratic" unions. A stable collective bargaining relationship is often ensured by strong union leaders.

CONTROLS OVER INTERNAL UNION AFFAIRS

The federal Labor-Management Reporting and Disclosure Act of 1959 (Landrum-Griffin Act) requires certain reports to the U.S. Department of Labor, Office of Labor-Management and Welfare-Pension Reports (LMWP). It regulates elections of union officers, trusteeships over union locals, and requires a bond for union officers. Most of this law is enforced by the LMWP, but the "bill of rights" for union members is enforced by the member filing a lawsuit in a federal district court. A member may also bring a lawsuit in a federal or state court under the "common law" or under other federal or state laws.

Every member of a union has equal rights to **Bill of rights** nominate candidates, to vote in elections of the union, to attend membership meetings, and to vote on union business, subject to reasonable rules and regulations in the union's constitution and bylaws. A member has the right at union meetings to express his views upon candidates for a union election, or other matters.

The rate for initiation fees, dues, and assessments may not be increased for a local except by majority vote by secret ballot by a membership referendum, or in a membership meeting after reasonable notice of intention to vote on the question. The rates for other unions, except an international or federation, may not be increased except by majority vote of delegates at a proper convention, by majority vote in a membership referendum, or by majority vote of the executive board if provided for in the constitution and bylaws.

A union cannot limit the right of a member to bring a lawsuit or appear as a witness in a court or before a government agency. However, before suing a union or union officers a member may be required to exhaust reasonable hearing procedures (but not to exceed a four-month period) within the union. A member may file a charge with the NLRB without waiting four months.

If the member pays the regular dues he cannot be fined, suspended, or otherwise disciplined by the union unless he has been served with written specific charges, given a reasonable time to prepare his defense, and afforded a full and fair hearing. Any provision in the union constitution or bylaws which is not consistent with this provision is of no force and effect.

The secretary or other officer of a local union is required to give a copy of the collective bargaining agreement to any member who requests it and whose rights are directly affected by it. If the union officer does not comply with this request the member should notify the nearest office of U.S. Department of Labor, LMWP.

Reports by unions and others   Each local, international, or other union is required to adopt a constitution and bylaws and to file it with the U.S. Department of Labor, LMWP, within 90 days after the union comes under this federal law. (See "How Labor Unions Are Organized," at page 3, for more information.) If a union is put under trusteeship by an international or other "parent" union, the parent union must file certain reports with the LMWP. Officers or employees of a union must prepare a report of certain economic interests which he or his spouse or minor child have in companies whose employees the union represents or seeks to represent, and payments to them made by a labor relations consultant to an employer. Employers and their labor consultants must prepare a report of certain payments or agreements to pay a union or any union officer.

As mentioned above, a union which assumes a **Trusteeships** trusteeship over another union must prepare a report within 30 days, and twice a year thereafter. A trusteeship can be imposed only for the purpose of correcting corruption or financial malpractice, assuring the bargaining duties of the union, restoring democratic procedures, or otherwise carrying out the lawful objects of the union.

It is unlawful to count the votes of delegates of a union under trusteeship in a convention of the parent union, unless the delegates have been selected in a secret ballot election in which all members in good standing of the union under trusteeship were allowed to vote. It is also unlawful to transfer to the parent union any current receipts or other funds of the union under trusteeship, except the normal per capita tax and assessments normally payable.

A trusteeship imposed after following the procedure stated in the constitution and bylaws, and authorized or ratified after a fair hearing before the executive board or similar body, is presumed to be valid for 18 months. After 18 months, the trusteeship is presumed to be invalid. The union under trusteeship, or any member of that union, may file a written complaint with the LMWP regional office. The LMWP may then file a lawsuit to end the trusteeship.

Elections of union officers

Elections of officers in national or international unions are required at least every five years, either by secret ballot among the members in good standing or at a convention of delegates chosen by secret ballot, in accordance with the constitution or by-laws, if they are not inconsistent with this part of the Landrum-Griffin Act. Each local must elect its officers at least every three years by secret ballot among its members in good standing. "Intermediate unions," such as joint boards or joint councils, must have an election at least every four years, among the members in good standing or by officers elected by members in good standing.

A candidate for office in a union election has the right to have the union distribute campaign literature "by mail or otherwise" at the candidate's expense. The union must give equal treatment to all candidates for election. Each candidate may make one inspection within 30 days before the election of a list of names and addresses of all members who are covered by a collective bargaining agreement having a requirement that employees join the union. The union must have safeguards to ensure a fair election, and each candidate may have an observer at the polls and at the counting of the ballots.

Each member in good standing is eligible to be a candidate and to hold office (subject "to reasonable qualifications uniformly imposed") and to vote for or support his candidate without being subjected to discipline or reprisal of any kind. At least 15 days before the election, each member must be mailed a copy of the election notice. Each member in good standing is eligible to one vote. If the employer has agreed to a checkoff of union dues, a member is not ineligible to vote or to be a candidate because of claimed delay or default in payment of dues. The election must be conducted in accordance with the constitution and bylaws of the union, if they are not inconsistent with this part of the Landrum-Griffin Act. For local union elections the votes cast and the results must be published separately.

Ballots, credentials of the delegates (if any), all minutes, and records of an election must be preserved for one year. No money received by a union by way of dues, assessments, or similar levy, or money from an employer, may be used to promote any candidate in a union election. However, money from dues or assessments may be used for notices of the election, for factual statements of issues not involving candidates, and other expenses of holding the election.

If a member believes that the union's constitution and bylaws do not provide an adequate procedure for the removal of a union officer guilty of serious conduct, the member may notify the regional office of the LMWP. The LMWP may schedule a hearing to determine whether the union's procedure for removal of officers is adequate. If it finds that the procedure is not adequate it may direct an election among the members in good standing on the issue whether the officer should be removed.

If an individual believes that the union of which he is a member has violated the election requirements of the Landrum-Griffin Act, he should attempt to correct the wrong by the procedure set up under the union constitution and bylaws. In many local unions this means filing a charge and its trial before the trial body of the local union, and appeal to the international. When the union makes a final decision which is not satisfactory to the member, within the next 30 days he may contact the regional office of the LMWP to file a complaint. If the union has made no final decision for three months after his first attempt under the constitution and bylaws to correct the wrong, the member may within 30 days file a complaint with the LMWP, or he can wait until the union takes final action, then within 30 days file a complaint.

If after investigation of the complaint the LMWP believes that violations have occurred which may have affected the election outcome, the LMWP will attempt to get the union to conduct a fair rerun election. If the union refuses, the LMWP may go to a federal district court to seek an order directing a rerun election.

Safeguards for unions   The law provides that the officers, agents, shop stewards, and other representatives of a union occupy positions of trust in relation to the union and its members as a group. They hold the union's money and property solely for the benefit of the union and its members. They are prohibited from dealing with the union in an adverse capacity or on behalf of an adverse party in any matter connected with their duties as officers. If it is claimed that any officer, agent, shop steward, or representative of the union has violated these duties and the union or its officers fail to take action to get appropriate relief after any member asks them to take action, then the member himself can sue for appropriate relief for the benefit of the union.

Any officer or employee of a union who embezzles or steals money or other property of the union may be fined up to $10,000 and sentenced to prison for up to five years.

If the total value of the property and yearly receipts of the union is more than $5,000 then a bond to protect against loss by fraud or dishonesty must cover each officer, agent, shop steward, representative, or employee of the union who handles union funds or other property.

A union cannot make a loan to any of its officers or employees which loan or loans outstanding total over $2,000. A violation of this section can be punished by a fine and prison sentence.

Miscellaneous provisions   It is unlawful to picket any employer for a purpose to enrich any individual, by taking any money or thing of value from that employer against his will. However, a union may picket for a "bona fide" increase in wages or other employee benefits. A violation can be punished by a $10,000 fine and 20 years in prison.

It is unlawful for any union or its officer, agent, shop steward, or other representative, or employee to fine, suspend, expel, or otherwise discipline any member for exercising any of his rights under this law. A member may sue in a federal district court for violation of these rights.

There are many types of lawsuits against unions. Some are based upon federal or state laws, and some are based upon "common law," or other decisions of the courts.

Lawsuits against unions

The most common court actions brought by employers against unions are actions for breach of a collective bargaining agreement, or actions for damages for a secondary boycott. Employers may also sue unions in state courts for damages caused during a strike.

Union members may sue their union under the "Bill of Rights" law, Title I of the federal Labor-Management Reporting and Disclosure Act of 1959 (the Landrum-Griffin Act). (See "Controls over Union Affairs," at page 57.)

In many states members may also sue their union in state courts for breach of the union's constitution and bylaws, a "contract" between the member and the union.

A union which is recognized by the employer as the exclusive bargaining agent has a duty to represent all employees in the bargaining unit fairly, whether or not they are members of the union. The union "recognized" by the employer has a duty to investigate grievances filed by employees in the bargaining unit. If the union believes the grievance has merit and may be taken to arbitration, the union has a duty to take it to arbitration, unless the employer offers a reasonable settlement of the dispute. However, if a union in good faith believes that a grievance does not have merit, or that the union would have little chance of winning if it should take the matter to arbitration, the union can properly refuse to process the grievance to arbitration.

A union which is the exclusive bargaining agent of employees has a duty to represent employees fairly, regardless of their race, color, national origin, religion, age or sex. If a union discriminates against employees the union may violate Title VII of the federal Civil Rights Act of 1964, as amended, or state laws prohibiting discrimination. The union may also violate other federal laws such as the Equal Pay Act of 1963 for sex discrimination or executive orders of the President. If a union discriminates against employees they may either file a complaint with a government agency or sue the union in court for damages caused by the discrimination.

COLLECTIVE BARGAINING

Labor negotiations When an employer recognizes a union as the representative of a majority of the employees in an "appropriate bargaining unit," the union usually asks the employer by letter to meet to negotiate a contract. (For a discussion of the appropriate unit, see "The Appropriate Bargaining Unit," at page 7.) In some industries, such as construction, the union usually asks the employer to sign a copy of its "standard agreement." In most industries, the union presents a complete proposed contract. The union and the company representatives then hold several meetings to discuss each item of the proposals.

If there has been a collective bargaining agreement, but changes are desired, the first step in negotiations is to be sure that all notices required by the old contract and by law have been given. The federal National Labor Relations Act, as amended, requires that a written notice to amend or terminate the contract be given to the other side at least 60 days before the termination or "automatic renewal" date of the old contract. A written notice must also be given to the Federal Mediation and Conciliation Service, 30 days before the termination or automatic renewal date. If the employer's state has a mediation service, written notice must be given to it at the same time. Any notice required by the contract must also be given, usually a written notice 60 to 90 days before the termination or automatic renewal date.

The union usually gives these notices, since employers may not desire any changes. If neither the union nor the employer gives the notice required by the contract, it may be automatically renewed for a one-year period. If neither the union nor the employer gives the notices to mediators, a strike or a lockout will probably be an unfair labor practice, and strikers can be terminated.

Negotiations differ a lot from one industry to another. In some industries, such as construction, it may consist only of the employer signing a copy of the standard area contract. Often only the paid business agents will represent the union at the bargaining table. An employee negotiation committee often assists a full-time union agent. Employers often bargain together in an association, and each employer is usually bound when an agreement is reached. The employers and the union each select a spokesman to do most of the talking. Sometimes the master agreement does not cover all of the wages and conditions of employment, and separate agreements are negotiated with the union for each employer to supplement the master agreement. If no agreement is reached in negotiations, the union can strike or the employer can lock out.

A mediator is usually an employee of a state or the federal government, who attempts to help the employer and the union reach an agreement. He meets with the parties jointly or separately to learn what items they disagree upon, what each side thinks is most important, and attempts to get one or both sides to change its proposal enough to reach an agreement. He can only make recommendations. Neither side is legally required to agree to his suggestions. The constitution of some international unions requires that a mediator be called into negotiations before the international will pay strike benefits to a local union or its members.

Collective bargaining agreements

Contracts vary a lot in different industries. Contracts also vary from one union to another. However, most contracts contain clauses granting to the union "exclusive recognition" among the named job classifications and locations; stating hours and days of work and overtime; how seniority is earned and how seniority and ability are used in promotions and layoffs; earning, taking and payment for vacations and holidays, sick leave and leaves of absence; filing and processing grievances and how a dispute may be taken to arbitration; the effective date of the contract, its duration, and a provision for terminating or "opening" the contract for changes. Many contracts include some form of "union security" (such as requiring union membership after 30 days' employment) and limit the right of the union to strike or of the employer to lock out.

If there is a hospital and medical plan, the contract usually names the plan and may state who is eligible and how much the employer pays each month, and refer to a booklet or the Trust Agreement for more information. If there is a retirement or other "benefit plans," such as for dental care, the contract usually names the plan and states the amount of payments, but refers to a booklet or the Trust Agreement for more information.

Employers and unions usually consider provisions in a contract to be a "noncost item" or a "cost item." Cost items include wages and various "fringe benefits." All cost items except wages are often called "fringe benefits."

Many unions in negotiations attempt to get an agreement with the employer on "language" for "noncost items" before making a serious effort to reach agreement on cost items. Noncost items include the clause stating that the employer recognizes the union as the agent for a named group of employees, rights reserved by management, union security, classifications of employees (such as probationary, temporary, regular, and part-time), seniority, promotions, and layoffs, work rules, safety rules, grievance and arbitration procedure, hiring hall procedures "no discrimination" clause, "savings clause" (providing that if part of the contract is ruled by a court or agency to be unlawful the balance of the contract remains in effect), the effective date for the beginning and the end of the contract, and the procedure to "open" the contract for changes or to terminate it.

Fringe benefits include pay for time not worked, such as rest or "coffee break" periods, paid lunch time, layover or reporting pay, vacations, holidays, sick pay, industrial accident pay, clean-up and checkout time, voting, jury duty, training, termination pay, layoff pay, and breakdown time.

"Cost" fringe benefits also include premium pay for time worked, such as overtime, Sunday, holiday, or weekend pay, shift premiums, and job differentials.

Miscellaneous "cost" fringe benefits include callback pay, health and welfare, prescription drugs insurance, dental care, vision care, retirement, profit sharing, life insurance, social security, workmen's compensation, unemployment insurance premiums, travel pay, board and lodging, moving expenses, and cost of making payroll deductions.

Thirty years ago there were few "cost fringes" in contracts. Many employees and unions considered them to be "paternalistic." But price controls during

World War II limited the amount of wage increases, and employers agreed to various fringe benefits, such as paid holidays and paid vacations, to give increased benefits to employees when "wages" were controlled. Decisions of the National Labor Relations Board and the courts also ruled that a union could insist that an employer bargain on fringe benefits, such as a retirement plan. Unions have also learned that employees may not be required to pay income taxes on most fringe benefits, but a wage increase subjects an employee to higher income taxes.

To be effective in negotiations one should know about what each fringe costs the employer in cents per hour. One should also know how many hours are normally worked per year by the group of employees who will be covered by the contract, and the average hourly wage rate. Then the employee can quickly compute the cost to the employer of each proposal, either in cents per hour, dollars per year, or a percentage increase in present costs.

The "common law of the shop"

You have probably heard of the "common law" of England and the United States. This has been developed over many years by custom and by court decisions, rather than by statutes passed by legislatures. There is also the "common law of the shop," dealing with the relation between employees, employers, and unions. This common law has developed by custom, decisions of arbitrators, by boards such as the National Labor Relations Board, and by court decisions.

One source of information about the "common law of the shop" is to examine the published decisions of arbitrators in labor cases, such as those published by the Bureau of National Affairs or the American Arbitration Association. Many large city libraries or law libraries maintain a set of these decisions. The decisions are often classified by subject or the issue involved in the dispute, such as discharge or discipline, promotions, transfers, lay-offs, severance pay, seniority, employee benefits, wages, overtime and premium pay, picketing and strikes, jurisdictional disputes, and management rights.

The total of customs, practices, and rules applying to employees of a particular employer might be called the "common law" of that employer. It tends to be fairly uniform in a particular industry. Any employee who has worked in industry learns "how things are done" where he is employed. Often many of the customs are not expressly stated in a union contract, contract interpretation manual, company policy manual for employees, or by printed rules passed out to employees or posted on a bulletin board. If a union agent is attempting to organize employees or to negotiate a first contract with an employer he usually has many meetings with employees to learn how things are done where they are employed.

Grievances

Nearly all union contracts have a procedure for handling disputes which arise during the term of the contract. Some contracts make any dispute which arises between an employee and the employer, or between the union and the employer, to be the subject of a grievance. Other contracts require an employer to discuss as a grievance only matters involving the interpretation or the application of the contract.

The procedure for handling a dispute varies, with some contracts providing for an elaborate procedure. At the first step the employee usually discusses the gripe or dispute with his immediate foreman. If he is not satisfied he may discuss his problem with a job steward (if the union has stewards), who is usually another employee. If there is no steward, the employee may discuss it with the union business agent, who is often a full-time, paid agent or officer of the union. If the steward or business agent believes the employee has a valid complaint, he will usually go with the complaining employee to discuss it with the next higher level of management.

In any discussion of a grievance, try to be sure of the "facts." If it involves a dispute over pay, for example, an employer may take the payroll records or an employee may take the paycheck stub for the last few pay periods with him. Each should take a copy of the contract. One should explain his position without arguing or losing patience. No one is always right. A grievance meeting should be mostly a discussion of the facts, at least at the first part of the meeting. The parties should see if they can agree on what happened. When they decide what happened, they should attempt to agree on the contract sections which are involved. The parties may still have an honest difference of opinion as to how the contract should be applied to the particular facts.

If the employee still does not agree, the union may decide that there has been a violation of the contract, and will take it up to the next step in the grievance procedure. The dispute should be written, with the complaining employee stating his version of what happened that caused the dispute to arise, and the contract sections believed to have been violated. The steward or business agent, and the foreman or supervisor, should each write on the grievance form what was discussed in the grievance meeting.

Most contracts provide that a grievance must be filed within a stated time period, such as seven days, after the event occurred. The contract usually states a time period within which the grievance must be "appealed" to the next step. If it is not appealed within that period the right to appeal may have been lost. However, some courts and arbitrators rule that a grievance may still be heard if the complaining employee or the union was not careless in their delay, or if they were absent for a while, or if they did not know about the event that caused the dispute.

If a matter can be made the subject of a grievance, such as the employer refusing to pay the wage rate or hours which an employee thinks is proper, the employee should go ahead and do the job assigned to him by the foreman. If the employee believes the foreman is wrong, the employee may, on time not paid for, consult the steward or the business agent to discuss whether to file a grievance. If an employee flatly refuses to do a job assigned to him, it might result in his being fired, even though the union believes that his interpretation of the contract is correct. Employees and the union should first do the job, then use the grievance procedure. If there is a strike or work stoppage over a matter that could be covered by a grievance, it may be an unlawful work stoppage.

An employee should not leave his work area during work time to investigate or get facts from other employees about a grievance, unless he has permission from his supervisor. Even if an employee has a valid grievance, but he abandons his job duties, he could properly be disciplined for that. Likewise a union steward should not leave his work area to investigate a grievance or to attend a grievance hearing unless the contract clearly gives him that right, or unless he has permission from his immediate supervisor or the proper company official. Even if the contract gives a steward the right to leave his job duties to handle a grievance, the steward should first notify his immediate supervisor.

Arbitration

If a grievance is not settled satisfactorily to the union, most contracts provide that the union may take it to arbitration. Some contracts also permit the employer to take the dispute to arbitration. While a union has a duty to fairly represent everyone in the bargaining unit, whether a member of the

union or not, and regardless of race or color, the
union is not required to take a grievance to arbitration if the union agents in "good faith" believe there
is little likelihood of winning before an arbitrator.

Arbitration is a procedure for a neutral person
or persons to interpret or apply a contract to a particular situation, and the decision is usually binding
on the employer and the union. (Compare this with
mediation, where neither the employer nor the union
is required to agree to suggestions of the mediator.)

The contract usually states how the arbitrator is
selected. Most contracts provide for one neutral arbitrator, but some contracts also provide for equal
numbers of one or two arbitrators for the employer
and one or two for the union. Some contracts provide for a committee of employer and union representatives to issue a decision which can be binding
on both sides. A few employers and unions which
have a large number of arbitration cases agree to a
"permanent" arbitrator or umpire for the duration
of the contract.

The contract usually provides for selection of a
neutral arbitrator, either from a list supplied by the
Federal Mediation and Conciliation Service, a federal
government agency, or by the American Arbitration
Association, a private organization. When the arbitrator is selected, a hearing is scheduled before him.
Sometimes the parties (usually the employer and
the union) are each represented by an attorney and
a court reporter is present to record everything that
is said. Such a hearing is similar to a court trial, but
is not as formal. The arbitrator usually permits witnesses to testify to matters and he will receive exhibits that a court would not permit. The main object of the arbitrator is to get the facts and apply
the contract to those facts.

In the hearing the arbitrator usually attempts to
get the parties to agree on exactly what the dispute
is about, to agree to the contract sections which

must be interpreted, and to agree to as many facts as they can. Evidence is received as to other grievances or arbitration decisions affecting the same section of the contract, what was said by the parties about the intent of those sections in grievance or other meetings, or in labor negotiations to change the language, and the "past practices" or how the employer has interpreted and applied that rule or contract section.

If briefs are permitted after the hearing, the parties may name and analyze decisions of the same arbitrator or other arbitrators interpreting similar rules or contract language. Decisions of arbitrators are published by several groups, including the Bureau of National Affairs and the American Arbitration Association. The bound or loose-leaf volumes may be found in a law library or in some city libraries.

An arbitrator has considerable authority to interpret and apply a contract to a particular situation, unless his authority is clearly limited by language in the contract or by a "stipulation" or other agreement by the parties. Employers and unions nearly always abide by the decision of an arbitrator, but his decision may be appealed to a court. The cost of arbitration, including the arbitrator's fee (about $200 a day), and the hearing room rental is usually shared equally by the employer and the union. Each side pays its own attorney's fee and the reporter's charge for the transcript.

If a dispute between a union and an employer may be taken to binding arbitration, a union cannot call or support a strike of employees on that matter. The union may take the matter to arbitration but cannot lawfully strike. Employees who strike may be terminated and the union can be sued by the employer for actual damages caused by the breach of contract, and the employer can ask a court to grant an injunction against the strike.

Court
enforcement of
collective
bargaining
agreements

A collective bargaining agreement is somewhat like any other contract. If there is a breach or violation of any of its terms the other party to the agreement — union or employer — may sue in court for breach of contract. However, if the contract has a clause providing for arbitration of any dispute over the interpretation of the contract, then a court will usually refuse to decide the dispute. A union and employer may be required to go to arbitration rather than to court.

If a union or employer refuses to use the procedure in the contract for arbitration, the other party may ask a court to order arbitration of the dispute. If a union or employer refuses to honor the decision of an arbitrator, the other party can ask a court for an order enforcing the arbitrator's award.

Federal law, as outlined in Section 301 of the National Labor Relations Act, as amended, must usually be followed in court actions to enforce a collective bargaining agreement. However, the lawsuit may be brought in a federal or a state court. Section 301 can also be used in a lawsuit over breach of an agreement by an employer to make payments to a labor-management pension plan trust. It can be used where a local union sues its parent international union for breach of the international's constitution.

If the contract has a clause stating that the union will not strike during the agreement, a court may issue an injunction against a threatened strike by the union.

LEGAL PROCEDURE

Our American court system is based upon rules of evidence copied from the English court system. The court rules attempt to permit a plaintiff and defendant a fair trial by keeping out testimony or documents which are untrustworthy. Government agencies, such as the National Labor Relations Board, in their hearings attempt to follow the court rules of evidence where practical.

If an employee plans to file a charge or complaint with a government agency or to sue an employer or union in court, or if he believes his collective bargaining agreement has been violated, he will have to convince someone that his position is correct. This means that the plaintiff must convince someone that his view of the facts is correct.

An employee's statement as to what happened will be more convincing if he keeps notes. A few lines showing the date, time of day, location, and who said what will refresh his memory at any later time, and will help make his story more convincing. If the employee keeps such a record for several weeks or months he can often win where there is a disagreement about what happened or what was said. He should also put the date on any business notes or letters he writes and keep a carbon copy or photocopy for himself.

If the dispute gets to trial or a hearing, the plaintiff or complaining party usually puts its "case" on first. The plaintiff calls individuals to testify as witnesses, to answer questions as to what he saw, did, heard, or said. Each witness on cross-examination may be asked questions by the other side, the defendant. In many hearings and in most trials a record is made as to what was said, either by a tape recording, a shorthand reporter, or by some other means. Documents and other objects are identified by witnesses and may be received into evidence as an exhibit.

When the plaintiff completes its "case in chief" the defendant puts on its case, by calling witnesses and introducing exhibits. Again, each witness is subject to cross-examination. When the defense "rests" the plaintiff may call witnesses or introduce documents to "rebut" points made by the defendant. The defendant may then answer with witnesses and exhibits. The hearing officer, jury, or judge is usually given power to find the facts and may have authority to make a decision.

If an individual is called as a witness, he will be more effective if he has sometime before considered the questions likely to be asked on "direct" examination and on cross-examination, and his answers to those questions. He should not try to memorize his answers. A witness should not argue with the questioner; he should control his temper. He should listen to the question; if he doesn't understand the question, he should say so and ask that it be rephrased or repeated. A witness should think before he answers; he should be helpful, not funny. Testimony is more likely to be believed if the witness is fair.

DISCRIMINATION IN EMPLOYMENT

Race, color, religion, national origin, and sex discrimination

The federal Equal Employment Opportunities Commission (EEOC) was established by the Civil Rights Act of 1964. It prohibits discrimination in employment based on race, color, religion, national origin, or sex. It applies to most employers with 15 or more employees, labor unions with 15 or more members, and to employment agencies, including state employment agencies.

About two thirds of the states have a state agency with authority to help an individual if he is discriminated against. Check the phone directory for the capital city or largest city for the address of the state agency and the address of the nearest federal EEOC office, or inquire at a state employment office or the state department of labor for the addresses.

If an individual believes he was not permitted to join a union, or he was not hired, not given a promotion, not admitted to apprentice training or other training, not properly paid, or was laid off or terminated because of his race, color, religion, national origin, or sex, he may file a charge.

A state agency may require that a charge be filed within less than 180 days after the act believed to be discrimination. If an individual waits more than 180 days it is probably too late. However, if an individual files only with the state agency he may have up to 300 days after the act he believes to be unlawful, to file a charge with the EEOC. The EEOC will send a copy of the charge to the employer or other party whom he claims discriminated. The "charged party" should begin to prepare a detailed statement why it is not guilty as charged.

Most state agencies will investigate the charge, and if the state finds evidence to believe there was discrimination, it will attempt to "remedy" the unlawful act, such as by causing an employer to promote the individual with back pay, or by causing a union hiring hall to stop preferring members of a particular race or color. If the charge is not settled satisfactorily the state agency will usually conduct a hearing, at which the individual filing the charge and other witnesses may testify. If the state's hearing officer finds there was discrimination in violation of the law his decision may be enforced by the state, or perhaps by the individual, in state courts. The party found to have discriminated can also appeal. There is usually no charge to an individual for filing and prosecuting a charge before a state agency, unless he decides to use a private attorney.

If the state agency has not investigated and settled the charge, usually within 60 days after it was filed with the state, the federal EEOC may then begin its investigation if the individual filed a charge with the EEOC.

The federal EEOC procedure is similar to that outlined above in state agencies. If the EEOC, after a hearing, finds that there was discrimination but the party found to have discriminated does not satisfactorily settle the matter, the government attorneys may sue to enforce the EEOC order in federal court. There is no cost to the individual for this service.

If the EEOC has not settled the matter within 180 days after filing a charge, the individual who filed the charge may request that the EEOC give to him a "suit letter." He may then within 90 days file a lawsuit in a federal district court. He may ask the court to appoint an attorney to represent him without the payment of any fees or costs. If the individual wins, the court may order him reinstated if he was fired from a job, or promoted if it finds he was wrongfully denied a promotion, and he may be granted back pay.

Many states have laws limiting the hours that women may work, requiring that women be paid overtime, providing a rest period morning and afternoon, or providing a lounge. Some "women's protective laws" also prohibit women from lifting heavy weights, or from doing particular jobs. Many state antidiscrimination agencies, the EEOC, or courts have ruled that such state laws discriminate against one sex and are invalid. Sometimes a ruling directs that the favored treatment (such as payment of overtime) be given to men as well as to women. In determining whether a woman is capable of performing a job, for example, the employer should consider whether the particular individual is qualified and not refuse to consider all women for the job.

Other legal action for discrimination

A union which is recognized by the employer as the "exclusive" representative of a group of employees, has a legal duty not to discriminate unfairly against any employee in that group. If, for example, such a union fails to insist upon the same wages for black employees or women as for men performing equal work, the union probably violates its duty. Any employee could file an unfair labor practice charge with the National Labor Relations Board against the union. If an employer agrees with a union on wages or working conditions which discriminate, for example, against blacks or women, the employer also may commit an unfair labor practice.

Some collective bargaining agreements have a clause prohibiting discrimination on the basis of race, color, religion, national origin, or sex. Many federal and state agencies require such a clause in collective bargaining agreements of companies with which they do business. If this clause is violated and the contract has another clause providing for arbitration, an employee covered by the contract may file a grievance protesting against such discrimination, and if necessary, take the grievance to arbitration. If the contract does not have an arbitration provision, an employee or the union may consult an attorney to discuss suing the employer in court for breach of the collective bargaining clause prohibiting discrimination.

If an individual believes that he is discriminated against at work or in not being hired because of his race, color, religion, national origin, or sex, he may consult a private attorney to discuss other possibilities. These include (1) a lawsuit claiming that his union is not representing him fairly in violation of the National Labor Relations Act (or if he is employed by a railroad or commercial airline, in violation of the Railway Labor Act), (2) a lawsuit claiming that his civil rights are violated in violation of several federal laws passed from 1866 to 1871, (3) filing a charge with a city human rights commission if his city has an antidiscrimination office, or (4) if the employer has contracts with a federal or state government agency an individual's attorney may check to see if that agency prohibits discrimination by its contractors.

The federal Equal Pay Act of 1963 changed the federal Wage and Hour Law to prohibit discrimination in wages because of sex for equal work on jobs which require equal skill, effort, and responsibility and which are performed under similar working conditions. If an individual believes this law is violated, he may contact the federal Wage and Hour office in the city nearest to him.

Discrimination because of age   The federal Age Discrimination in Employment Act of 1967 protects individuals ages 40 through 64 against discrimination in employment because of age. It prohibits classified advertising for a "young" applicant. Employers, unions, and employment agencies are covered by this law. A seniority system may be lawful even though it tends to favor older employees. If an individual believes that this law is violated, he may contact the federal Wage and Hour Division in the city nearest to him within 180 days after the act believed to be discrimination occurred.

Many states also have a law prohibiting discrimination in employment because of ages 40 through 64. The state agency which prohibits other discrimination in employment often also enforces the law which prohibits age discrimination. For more information look in the telephone directory of the state's capital city or the largest city for the address of this agency, or ask the state employment office for information. An individual may file a charge of age discrimination with both his state agency and the federal Wage and Hour Division. The federal agency will usually wait for the state agency to investigate.

INDUSTRIAL ACCIDENT AND OCCUPATIONAL DISEASE INSURANCE

All states have a law providing for compensation for employees injured at work. In many states the employer pays the entire cost of this insurance, but in other states the employee pays part of the cost. In some states the insurance may be provided by a private insurance company, or larger employers may "self-insure," or a state agency may provide the insurance.

In most states, if an employee is injured at work or while performing an errand for his employer, he cannot sue his employer in court for injuries, but the employee is limited to benefits under industrial accident insurance (workmen's compensation). If an individual's state does not require an employer to provide this insurance for employees (farm workers, domestic workers, and employees of nonprofit occupations may not be covered), an employee may sue his employer in court for injuries.

If an individual is permanently and totally disabled from an accident occurring at work he may receive a percentage of his wages each month for the rest of his life, and upon his death his wife and other dependents may be entitled to continued benefits. The regular disability payments if an individual is single equal about 50 or 60 percent of his wages, and a greater amount if he has dependents.

If an individual dies as a result of an accident occurring at work his dependents are entitled to regular monthly payments. Monthly death benefits for his dependents are about the same as disability benefits. In many states burial expenses of up to several hundred dollars will be paid by industrial insurance.

State industrial accident insurance also provides a regular monthly payment for the rest of an employee's life if he is permanently but only partially disabled from an accident at work. In some instances, such as the loss of a limb, he will receive a lump-sum payment. For each of the above accidents at work, the individual's doctor, hospital, and other medical expenses will be paid by industrial accident insurance.

Many states operate rehabilitation facilities to train injured workers to enable them to return to work. This may include physical therapy to restore physical ability, or it may include vocational training to learn to do a different job. The costs are usually paid by the industrial insurance. If an individual is injured his doctor may recommend that he receive this training.

Occupational disease coverage is provided in most states. If an individual becomes ill because of exposure over a long period of time to hazards such as lead poisoning, dust diseases, or radiation, he may be entitled to benefits. The individual should see a physician as soon as he has symptoms and file a claim with the state agency or insurance company which insures the employer. Some states require that an individual file a claim within six months or so after the illness, or he may lose his right to benefits.

If an individual is injured at work he should report it to his supervisor and see that a written accident report is prepared. If the injury affects an individual's ability to work he should see a doctor and ask him to help file a claim. The employer may provide the address of the state industrial accident agency or the individual may look in the telephone directory for the address, and ask for help in filing a claim.

If an individual's claim for an injury or occupational disease is denied he may consult a private attorney as soon as possible to decide whether to appeal his claim.

An employer should check with the agency or company which provides his insurance to determine if supervisors and other management personnel are covered by the insurance. They can usually be included at a low cost.

UNEMPLOYMENT INSURANCE

The state employment offices, working with the federal government, administer a plan of unemployment insurance. In many states the entire cost of this insurance is paid by employers as a percentage of the employee's earnings. If an employer has a higher rate of labor turnover (hires, layoffs, terminations, and quits) his "experience rating" will be higher and his insurance costs may be greater.

If an employee works enough weeks in his "base period," usually a year, he is entitled to weekly benefits of about one half of his wages, for up to 26 weeks or more. Most states have a maximum weekly payment of about $75, but they may pay more for dependents.

An individual must be eligible for and seeking other employment to receive benefits in most states. If an individual believes that he is eligible for benefits he should report to his local state employment office, file a claim, and follow instructions concerning dates to report to their office. That office will probably ask for the name and address of his last employer, the date he last worked, the reason he is no longer working there, and his total earnings for the last calendar week he worked there. An individual should take his last paycheck stub if he has it.

If an individual is denied benefits the employment office will instruct him how to file an appeal. It must usually be filed in writing within a stated number of days after benefits are denied.

There is usually a waiting period of a week for benefits, or more if an individual voluntarily quit or was terminated for cause.

Supervisors and other management officials are usually eligible for unemployment benefits.

VETERANS' EMPLOYMENT RIGHTS

Federal laws and many state laws protect the right of an individual to return to a job which he left to enter military service. Some laws also permit members of the Armed Reserves or the National Guard to take time off without pay to attend required meetings or training courses. A veteran usually must have satisfactorily completed his active duty military service; a "bad conduct" or "undesirable" discharge is not satisfactory. The veteran must reapply for a job within 90 days after his release from active duty. If he was in active military status over four years he may not have a right to return.

The job which the veteran left must be "other than temporary." However, if he was a probationary or a part-time employee working fairly regularly, he is usually entitled to a job.

A veteran is usually entitled to pay increases which he would have had if he had not left to enter military service. He may be entitled to promotions he would have received, if it is reasonably certain that he would hold the higher job if he had not been in military service. However, if the higher job requires special training, such as apprentice training, he may be required to complete the training. A veteran earns seniority in the military service if he would have earned seniority if he had remained on the job.

For more information on employment rights for veterans, the individual may contact the federal or state employment office in his city, the state department of labor, the office of his state attorney general, or a private attorney. If an individual believes his former employer has refused to take him back, contrary to federal law, he may contact the nearest office of the U.S. attorney. This office is usually located in the federal courthouse building.

SOCIAL SECURITY

This federal insurance system includes old age, survivors, disability, and hospital (Medicare) and doctor's care (Medicaid) insurance. Half of the social security cost is paid for by deductions from an employee's wages and half is paid for by his employer. In 1972, deductions were 5.2 percent for each on the first $9,000 of earnings. Beginning in 1973, 5.85 percent is deducted on the first $10,800 of earnings. In 1974, deductions will be made on the first $12,000 of earnings. Benefits have been greatly increased, so social security is now a government pension plan, with costs and benefits greater than in most private pension plans. Almost all workers except some railroad and federal government employees are covered by social security.

When an individual reaches age 65 he may be eligible for monthly retirement benefits, or if he retires at age 62 he can get a lower amount each month. Males or females may retire at age 62.[1] The amount of the monthly payment is based on the individual's average earnings under social security and the number of years the deductions are made. An individual can continue to work past 65 but the amount of his monthly payment when he reaches age 65 may be reduced until he reaches age 72.

An individual must have a certain amount of credit for work covered by social security before he receives monthly payments. Consult the local social security office for the amount needed. In general, he will receive a quarter of a year credit for each quarter of a year when he earns $50 or more. Self-employed individuals with self-employment income of $400 a year or more get four quarters of credit.

If an individual is physically or mentally disabled and apparently unable to work for 12 months or longer, he may be entitled after a few months' waiting period, to monthly disability payments, even though he is much younger than 65. If he has a dependent wife, husband, or child, the amount of his monthly retirement or disability payment will usually be more than for a single person.

If the husband (or wife) dies, even before age 62, the survivor and dependent children may be entitled to monthly benefits for many years. The survivors may also be entitled to the cost of the burial.

If an individual believes he is eligible for social security payments he should contact his local social

---

[1]In this paragraph, and throughout this book, the terms "he," "his," or "him" are used for simplicity to apply to both sexes.

security office to apply for the payments. Look in the telephone directory for the address. Payments are not made automatically when an individual becomes eligible. He will need his social security number, and proof of age, such as a birth certificate. If an individual is applying for wife's or widow's benefits, she should take her marriage certificate. An individual may need his Form W-2 and tax statement, or if he is self-employed, his income tax return for last year.

If an individual is 65 or over and entitled to monthly payments he may be entitled to hospital insurance (Medicare) or medical insurance (Medicaid). An individual may be eligible for this insurance if he is 65 even though he is not eligible for monthly payments. An individual must enroll for the insurance at the social security office.

Hospital insurance pays for up to 90 days of hospital care in a "benefit period" but an individual must pay the first $72. After 60 days of hospital care he must pay about $18 for each day in the hospital. He also has a "lifetime reserve" of 60 more hospital days. If an individual needs nursing home care after hospital care, the insurance may pay all of the cost for the first 20 days, and all but about $9 per day of the cost for the next 80 days. An individual may also be eligible for visits to his home by nurses, physical therapists, or other health workers.

The hospital insurance is paid by a portion of the deductions from wages and by an equal payment by the employer.

The medical insurance pays 80 percent of the "reasonable" charges for physicians' services no matter where an individual receives the services, but he must usually pay the first $60 each year. It also pays 80 percent of the charge for other health services in the home if ordered by the doctor, and it pays 80 percent of many other medical services.

If an individual eligible for monthly social security benefit payments, wants the medical insurance, he will usually have the premium of $6.30 each month automatically deducted from his monthly benefit check. If he does not want this optional medical insurance he must notify the social security office.

PENSIONS

A pension plan usually provides for monthly benefit payments after an individual reaches a particular age and no longer works full time. Private or non-governmental plans are usually planned to qualify as exempt under income tax laws. If a pension plan is "qualified," the employer may deduct from its income tax the payments made to the plan on behalf of employees. The payments made by an employer under a qualified plan are not taxable to individual employees when the payments are made. Likewise, income to the pension plan from its investments are not taxable. When an individual receives benefits under a plan paid for by the employer those benefits are taxable, but the individual has usually retired then and has little income, thus little or no income tax need be paid.

Pension plans may be divided into several types. In many plans an individual eligible for benefits gets a stated amount per month, usually based upon the amount of payments per hour or per month paid on his behalf, or the number of years for which payments were made. In other plans regular reports are made of the value of the individual account of each employee; this value fluctuates as the value of the plan's investments fluctuates and as more payments are made for the employee.

Profit sharing plans usually involve a payment by the employer of an agreed-upon part of its profits to the plan on behalf of employees who participate in the plan; if there are no profits there are no payments.

In some pension plans the employee pays the entire cost of the plan. In "contributory" plans the employee contributes part of the cost, usually by deduction of a stated amount from the paycheck, and the employer pays the balance of the cost. Some plans permit an employee to make additional contributions to his account up to a stated amount; this may serve as a savings plan with interest or dividend earnings tax free until he retires.

In many plans a legal trust is established to receive the payments and to invest them in assets to earn money. Trustees may be established to determine how to invest the money in the fund. Most plans also have a committee or trustees to determine who is eligible to have payments made on his behalf under the plan, and to determine when individuals are eligible to receive retirement or other benefits.

One advantage of a properly established trust plan is that the fund of money paid in for pensions is separate from the employer's business. Creditors of the employer cannot receive money from the fund; it is reserved for pensions.

Payments made on behalf of an employee may "vest" or give the employee a legal right to a portion of the payments. Under some pension plans the payments become "fully vested" after a stated number of years for which payments are made. The right to benefits under other plans becomes fully vested after some formula is met, usually a combination of the number of years in which payments are made and the employee's age. An employee's right to benefits may vest under a formula such as 10 percent each year, and become fully vested after 10 years.

Sometimes a group or association of employers establishes a pension plan for employees of all employers covered by the plan. Many unions and employer associations have established a pension trust plan. The National Labor Relations Act, as amended, in Section 302, permits payments by an employer to such a plan if there are an equal number of labor trustees and employer trustees and if certain other requirements are met.

If a pension plan covers an association of employers, an employee may leave one employer and begin employment with another employer covered by the same pension plan, without loss of benefits and he may continue to earn benefits with the new employer. Some pension plans also have an agreement for "reciprocity" of benefits with another plan, so that an employee can get credit for his benefits earned under the other plan.

If an individual is over 40 years of age, he should estimate how much his monthly payments will be under any pension plan, and under federal social security. He can ask the administrator of his pension plan for help in computing benefits. His local social security office can help him in estimating the amount of social security benefits to which he may be entitled.

See "Social Security," for a summary of retirement and other benefits under social security, which is now a government pension plan for almost all workers.

OCCUPATIONAL SAFETY AND HEALTH ACT OF 1970

This law requires that each employer furnish to each of his employees employment "free from recognized hazards . . . likely to cause death or serious physical harm to his employees." It sets up a procedure to establish occupational safety and health standards for all industries. Employees or their union may request that the Secretary of Labor appoint an advisory committee to establish safety rules. If an employer applies for a variance from a standard his employees may participate in a hearing on that request, and may appeal from an order granting any variance.

All safety and health standards must provide for the use of labels or other warnings, such as posters, to notify employees of all hazards to which they are exposed, the symptoms, emergency treatment, and any required equipment to protect against a hazard.

An employee or the union agent representing employees may request that the Occupational Safety and Health Agency of the U.S. Department of Labor (OSHA) send an agent to make a physical inspection of the work area, if they believe that a violation of a standard exists that threatens serious harm or is an imminent danger. The complaining party may appeal the OSHA's refusal to make the inspection to the OSHA regional administrator. The appeal must be in writing with a copy sent by certified mail to the employer. The employer may send to the regional administrator a written statement opposing the inspection with a copy sent by certified mail to the complaining party. The regional administrator may conduct a hearing before making a decision.

Employees or their union agent may go with the OSHA agent in his inspection, and employees have the right to talk with him in private.

If an employee is discharged or otherwise discriminated against because he made a complaint to the OSHA agent about a hazard, the employee may within 30 days notify the OSHA, which may bring a court action for reinstatement with back pay.

If the OSHA agent finds a violation of a safety or health standard, the OSHA issues a citation, listing the hazard. The citation must be "promptly posted" by the employer. If the hazard is not corrected, the OSHA may schedule a hearing before a hearing officer, who will later issue a report determining whether a civil or criminal penalty should be assessed upon the employer. A three-member Occupational Safety and Review Commission is established for appeals from decisions of a hearing officer.

Employers are required to keep records of exposure by employees to poisonous or harmful materials, and they must promptly notify any employee who has been or is being exposed at levels greater than the amount listed in the standard. The employer must also notify employees of steps taken to reduce the hazard. The Secretary of Health, Education, and Welfare will prepare and keep an up-to-date list of poisonous substances. Employees will be permitted to see a copy of that list.

For more information, phone, write, or visit the U.S. Department of Labor in Washington, D.C. or in the city nearest to the employee.

In some states, OSHA has approved a state agency to make safety and health inspections. If one lives in a state with an "approved" law, his state agency will make the inspection. Look in the local telephone directory or the nearest city for the address, or contact the state employment office for the address.

WELFARE AND PENSION PLANS DISCLOSURE ACT

The federal law requires that the administrator of each pension, health, or life insurance plan covering 25 or more participants, prepare a description of the plan. An annual financial report, showing eligibility for benefits, contributions, expenses, and assets, is required for plans with more than 100 participants. A bond may be required of the administrator and all employees of the plan. Records, such as vouchers and receipts, made in administering the plan must be kept for five years.

If an individual is covered by such a plan he may request in writing from the administrator a description of the plan and a summary of the latest annual report. The administrator must file two copies of the plan and annual financial report with the Office of Labor-Management and Welfare-Pension Reports, U.S. Department of Labor. Individuals may examine the reports in their Public Documents Room, 8701 Georgia Avenue, Silver Spring, Maryland 20910, or individuals may write to them for a copy at a cost of 25 cents per page. Be sure to state the full name and address of the plan, name and address of the company or union, and type of employees covered by the plan (such as hourly or salaried).

The Department of Labor does not regulate such plans, interfere in plan management, interpret plan provisions, or assist in collecting benefits. To collect benefits under the plan, consult the plan administrator. An individual may also consult an attorney if he is denied benefits which he believes he is entitled to.

LAWS REQUIRING MINIMUM WAGES AND OVERTIME

Federal Wage and Hour Law This law, in general, requires that an employer pay a minimum wage of $1.60 an hour, and that he pay a rate of at least time and one-half for hours worked over 40 in a week. It applies to nearly all employees of most employers who are engaged in "interstate commerce." It also applies to particular employees of a small or large employer whose work involves the production, shipment, or receiving of goods which have moved or which the employer expects to move in interstate commerce. It applies to most employees of state and local governments, but does not apply to agricultural laborers. The Equal Pay Act of 1963 amended the minimum wage section of the law to prohibit paying of a lower wage to either sex for equal work on jobs which, to perform, requires equal skill, effort, and responsibility, and under similar working conditions.

There are many exemptions from coverage under the Wage and Hour Law. Motion-picture, theater employees, outside sales people, and the "white-collar jobs" of administrative, executive, and professional employees, including teachers, are exempted. Many small, local employers are not covered.

Others exempted from the overtime requirement include hotel, motel, and restaurant workers, taxi drivers, and local transportation company operating employees, most railroad, airline, and interstate trucking employees, and many employees of agricultural-related industries. Other seasonal employees in agricultural-related processing work may be exempted for 10-, 14-, or 20-week periods; during these periods they must be paid overtime only after 50 hours or in some cases, 48 hours, a week.

Restrictions are placed on "industrial homework" or work done in the home for an employer, which could otherwise be used to avoid the payment of the minimum wage or overtime.

Exempted from the federal Wage and Hour Law minimum wage requirement are learners, apprentices, and handicapped employees, and students in some jobs. A certificate may be required to pay the lower wage rate. Agricultural employees covered by the act may be paid $1.30 an hour rather than $1.60. Employees who regularly receive tips may be paid a lower hourly rate.

Child labor is prohibited in hazardous or detrimental work, for workers under age 18. Employment of children under 16 is prohibited except for a parent or guardian or where a certificate has been issued approving the particular work for the minor. An individual may inquire about how to get such a "work permit" from the federal or state wage and hour office near him, or from the school principal.

There is a two-year statute of limitations for violations of the law, but it is three years where the employer willfully violated the law. If an individual files a complaint with the federal wage and hour office and it decides there was a violation which is not settled, that office will represent the individual without cost to him, and it will attempt to get the amount which it believes the employer should have paid. An individual may see a private attorney to sue the employer for double the amount owed, and he may get the attorney's fee for his appearance in court, but perhaps not for his charge for investigating the case and preparing for trial.

State wage and hour laws   Many states have a law similar to the federal Wage and Hour Law, requiring the payment of time and one-half for time worked over 40 hours a week. Some state laws also apply to work over 8 hours per day. The state minimum wage is sometimes higher than the federal minimum wage. If both the federal and the state law apply, the employer must meet the requirements of both laws. State laws usually include restrictions on the employment of minors for hazardous work, or during school hours. States usually require minors under age 15 or 16 to attend school when it is in session.

Many state overtime and minimum wage laws apply only to women and minors. These laws may be found to discriminate on the basis of sex, and may be contrary to the state or federal law prohibiting such discrimination. A state law applying only to women may be "invalid," or courts may rule that it also applies to men.

Some states will help an employee collect unpaid wages due, especially if failure to make the payment violated the state's minimum wage or overtime law. For more information about the state's wage and hour law, an individual may phone or write his state department of labor.

Federal Public Contracts Act   The Walsh-Healy (Public Contracts) Act applies to the employees of most employers who have contracts to sell goods to or perform services for the federal government. This law requires payment of time and one-half for hours over 40 per week or 8 per day, and it requires payment of a rate not less than the wage "prevailing" in the industry, which must be at least the federal wage.

Labor by boys under 16 or girls under 18 years of age cannot be used under this law. Goods cannot be made at the worker's home, except for certain handicapped workers for sheltered workshops. Safety and health standards have been prepared for many types of work done on federal contracts.

If a violation is found the employer may be required to pay to the federal government $10 per day for each minor wrongfully employed, plus the amount of the underpayment to the employee. The government may cancel its contract with any supplier found to be in violation of this law, and that employer may be "blacklisted" or be unable to be awarded another government contract for three years.

For more information about this law, consult the nearest office of the U.S. Department of Labor, Wage and Hour and Public Contracts Division.

Federal Service Contract Act

This law is similar to the federal Public Contracts Act, but it applies to employers who contract to provide laundry, dry cleaning, janitorial work, guard service, food and cafeteria service, and similar services for the federal government. It requires the payment of the prevailing rate of wages, including fringe benefits, in the area, but not less than the minimum wage.

The government may withhold the amount of the unpaid wages from its payments to the contractor. The government may also cancel the contract, sue the contractor for the unpaid wages, or blacklist the contractor by making it ineligible for government contracts for three years.

For more information about this law, consult the nearest office of the U.S. Department of Labor, Wage and Hour and Public Contracts Division, or the head of the federal agency which let the contract.

Federal Work Hours Standards Act of 1962

This law applies to laborers and mechanics employed on construction jobs for the federal government. It requires the payment of time and one-half for hours in excess of 8 per day or 40 per week worked under such a government contract.

The government may levy a penalty of $10 per day for each employee who was not properly paid, plus the amount owing, and it may deduct this total amount due from payments by the government to the contractor. Some courts have ruled that an employee may sue his contractor for the amounts owing.

For more information about this law, consult the nearest office of the U.S. Department of Labor, Wage and Hour and Public Contracts Division.

Federal Davis-Bacon Act

This law applies to laborers and mechanics employed on construction jobs for the federal government. It usually applies only to work done on the construction site. This law requires the payment of the prevailing wages and fringe benefits in the area for work in the job classifications involved. The U.S. Department of Labor investigates and determines what it finds to be the wages and fringe benefits prevailing to the area, and it makes these findings available to contractors.

The government may withhold any amount owing to employees from payments to the contractor on this contract or other contracts with the government.

For more information about this law, consult the head of the government agency which let the contract, or the U.S. Department of Labor, Wage and Hour and Public Contracts Division.

Other state wage and hour laws

Many states have a law which requires payment of wages to employees in "lawful money" or checks but not in script or commodities. Two or more paydays may be required each month. Payment is often required within a stated number of hours or days after an employee quits or is terminated. A written statement listing all deductions may be required. No deductions may be permitted unless the employee authorizes them in writing or unless they are required by law.

Many states have a law patterned after the federal Davis-Bacon and Work Hours Standards laws. These state laws usually apply to construction work done for the state, and require payment of the prevailing wage rate, and time and one-half for hours worked in excess of 8 per day or 40 per week.

For more information about state wage and hour laws, contact the state department of labor or a private attorney.

A writ of garnishment is an order to someone who owes the individual something to pay that debt to the person who began the garnishment proceeding, rather than to him.

Wage garnishment laws

Most states have a law limiting the ability of an employee's creditors to garnish wages owed to him by an employer.

If an employee is not about to leave the state and has not removed property to defraud his creditors, he may have the right to a court hearing before any garnishment. State statutes usually limit the amount of an employee's wages which can be garnished.

The state statute or court decisions frequently limit the ability of an employer to terminate an employee for garnishments, at least, if the employee's wages are only garnished about once a year. For more information about state laws dealing with garnishment, consult a private attorney.

A federal statute also limits the garnishment of wages. This law limits the portion of an employee's wages which can be garnished. It also prohibits an employer from firing an employee for a first garnishment for a debt. For more information, consult a private attorney, the Legal Aid Services, or the U.S. Department of Labor, Wage and Hour Division. Check the local telephone directory for the address.

Government controls of wages and salaries

In August 1971, the federal government "froze" all wages and salaries for a 90-day period. This was known as "Phase I." By another Executive Order, effective November 14, 1971, wages and salaries were controlled by "Phase II."

Under Phase II, a Pay Board was established with five public members. It established "guidelines" permitting a maximum pay increase in a year to 5½ percent, plus up to 0.7 percent more for "fringe benefits." This was the overall increase for a unit of employees, such as a department; individual employees could receive more. Later, the wage controls were amended to apply only to employers with 60 or more employees, plus a few exceptions.

In the construction industry for employees represented by a union, the Construction Industry Stabilization Committee (CISC), consisting of four public, four labor, and four employer representatives, requires notification of all proposed wage and "fringe cost" increases before they are effective. Nonunionized construction employees were covered by the Pay Board. The CISC has delegated some of its authority to craft dispute boards, consisting of labor and management representatives in the particular construction craft. None of the proposed increases can be put into effect until it is approved.

Early in 1973, "Phase III" of wage and price controls was established. This removed most of the strict controls, except in the food, health care, and construction industries. General guidelines of 5½ percent for wage increases were maintained.

The detailed plan of wage and salary controls changes from time to time. For the current status of controls, check the newspaper or phone the local Internal Revenue Service office.

OFFICES OF THE NATIONAL LABOR RELATIONS BOARD

Region 1 — Boston, Mass., 02114 — 7th Floor, Bulfinch Bldg., 15 New Chardon St., Tel.: 223-3330

Region 2 — New York, N.Y., 10007 — 36th Floor, Federal Bldg., 26 Federal Plaza, Tel.: 264-0331

Region 3 — Buffalo, N.Y., 14202 — 9th Floor, Federal Bldg., 111 West Huron St., Tel.: 842-3100

Resident Office — Albany, N.Y., 12207 — 11th Floor, Standard Bldg., 112 State St., Tel.: 472-2215

Region 4 — Philadelphia, Pa., 19107 — 1700 Bankers' Sec. Bldg., Walnut and Juniper Sts., Tel.: 597-7601

Region 5 — Baltimore, Md., 21201 — Room 1019, Federal Bldg., Charles Center, Tel.: 962-2822

Region 6 — Pittsburgh, Pa., 15222 — 1536 Federal Bldg., 1000 Liberty Ave., Tel.: 644-2977

Region 7 — Detroit, Mich., 28226 — Room 500, Book Bldg., 1249 Washington Blvd., Tel.: 226-3200

Region 8 — Cleveland, Ohio, 44199 — Room 1695, Federal Office Bldg., 1240 East 9th St., Tel.: 522-3715

Region 9 — Cincinnati, Ohio, 45202 — Room 2407, Federal Office Bldg., 550 Main St., Tel.: 684-3688

Region 10 — Atlanta, Ga., 30308 — 730 Peachtree St., N.E., Tel.: 526-5760

Resident Office — Birmingham, Ala., 35203 — 1417 City Federal Bldg., 2026 2nd Ave., North, Tel.: 325-3877

Region 11 — Winston-Salem, N.C., 27101 — 1624 Wachovia Bldg., 301 North Main St., Tel.: 723-2300

Region 12 — Tampa, Fla., 33602 — Room 706, Federal Office Bldg., 500 Zack St., Tel.: 228-7227

Resident Offices — Miami, Fla., 33130 — Room 826, Federal Office Bldg., 51 S.W. First Ave., Tel.: 350-5391

Jacksonville, Fla., 32202 — Federal Building, 400 West Bay St., Tel.: 791-2168

Region 13 — Chicago, Ill., 60604 — Room 881, Everett McKinley Dirksen Bldg., 219 South Dearborn St., Tel.: 828-7572

Subregion 38 — Peoria, Ill., 61602 — 10th Floor, Savings Center Tower, 411 Hamilton Blvd., Tel.: 673-9282

Region 14 — St. Louis, Mo., 63102 — Room 448, North 12th Blvd., Tel.: 622-4167

Region 15 — New Orleans, La., 70113 — T6024 Federal Bldg., 701 Loyola Ave., Tel.: 527-6361

Region 16 — Fort Worth, Tex., 76102 — 8A24 Federal Office Bldg., 819 Taylor St., Tel.: 334-2921

Region 17 — Kansas City, Mo., 64106 — 610, Federal Bldg., 601 E. 12th St., Tel.: 334-2921

Region 18 — Minneapolis, Minn., 55401 — 316, Federal Bldg., 110 So. 4th St., Tel.: 725-2611

Region 19 — Seattle, Wash., 98101 — 10th Floor, Republic Bldg., 1511 Third Ave., Tel.: 442-4532

Subregion 36 — Portland, Ore., 97605 — Room 310, Six Ten Broadway Bldg., 610 S.W. Broadway, Tel.: 221-3085

Region 20 — San Francisco, Calif., 94102 — 13018 Federal Bldg., 450 Golden Gate Ave., Box 36047, Tel.: 556-3197

Subregion 37 — Honolulu, Hawaii, 96814 — Suite 308, 1311 Kapiolani Blvd., Tel.: 546-5100

Region 21 — Los Angeles, Calif., 90014 — Eastern Colombia Bldg., 849 South Broadway, Tel.: 688-5200

Region 22 — Newark, N.J., 07102 — 16th Floor, Federal Bldg., 970 Broad St., Tel.: 645-2100

Region 23 — Houston, Tex., 77002 — 4th Floor, Dallas-Brazos Bldg., 1125 Brazos St., Tel.: 226-4296

Region 24 — Hato Rey, P.R. — 7th Floor, Pan American Bldg., 225 Ponce De Leon Ave., Mailing Address: P.O. Box UU, Tel.: 622-2424

Region 25 — Indianapolis, Ind., 46204 — 614 ISTA Center, 150 W. Market St., Tel.: MElrose 3-8921

Region 26 — Memphis, Tenn., 38103 — 746, Federal
Office Bldg., 167 N. Main St., Tel.: 534-3161
Resident Offices — Little Rock, Ark., 72201 — 3511
Federal Bldg., 700 W. Capitol Ave., Tel.: 378-5512
Nashville, Tenn., 37203 — 403, West End Bldg.,
1720 West End Ave., Tel.: 749-5922
Region 27 — Denver, Colo., 80202 — Room 260, Fed-
eral Bldg., U.S. Custom House, 721 19th St., Tel.:
837-3551
Region 28 — Albuquerque, N.M., 87101 — 7011, Fed-
eral Bldg., U.S. Courthouse, 500 Gold Ave., S.W.,
Tel.: 843-2508
Resident Offices — Phoenix, Ariz., 85013 — Room
207, Camelback Bldg., 110 W. Camelback Rd.,
Tel.: 261-3717
El Paso, Tex., 79901 — Room 1205, The Mills
Bldg., 303 North Oregon, Tel.: 533-5381
Region 29 — Brooklyn, N.Y., 11201 — 4th Floor, 16
Court St., Tel.: 596-3535
Region 30 — Milwaukee, Wis., 53203 — 2nd Floor,
Commerce Bldg., 744 North Fourth St., Tel.: 224-
3861
Region 31 — Los Angeles, Calif., 90024 — Room
12100, Federal Bldg., 11000 Wilshire Blvd., Tel.:
824-7351

PETITION FOR CERTIFICATION OF REPRESENTATIVES

Form NLRB-502 (11-64)	UNITED STATES OF AMERICA NATIONAL LABOR RELATIONS BOARD	Form Approved. Budget Bureau No. 64-R002.14

PETITION

	DO NOT WRITE IN THIS SPACE
INSTRUCTIONS.—Submit an original and four (4) copies of this Petition to the NLRB Regional Office in the Region in which the employer concerned is located. If more space is required for any one item, attach additional sheets, numbering item accordingly.	CASE NO.
	DATE FILED

The Petitioner alleges that the following circumstances exist and requests that the National Labor Relations Board proceed under its proper authority pursuant to Section 9 of the National Labor Relations Act.

1. Purpose of this Petition *(If box RC, RM, or RD is checked and a charge under Section 8(b)(7) of the Act has been filed involving the Employer named herein. the statement following the description of the type of petition shall not be deemed made.)*
(Check one)

[X] RC-CERTIFICATION OF REPRESENTATIVES—A substantial number of employees wish to be represented for purposes of collective bargaining by Petitioner and Petitioner desires to be certified as representative of the employees.

[ ] RM-REPRESENTATION (EMPLOYER PETITION)—One or more individuals or labor organizations have presented a claim to Petitioner to be recognized as the representative of employees of Petitioner.

[ ] RD-DECERTIFICATION—A substantial number of employees assert that the certified or currently recognized bargaining representative is no longer their representative.

[ ] UD-WITHDRAWAL OF UNION SHOP AUTHORITY—Thirty percent (30%) or more of employees in a bargaining unit covered by an agreement between their employer and a labor organization desire that such authority be rescinded.

[ ] UC-UNIT CLARIFICATION—A labor organization is currently recognized by employer, but petitioner seeks clarification of placement of certain employees: *(Check one)* [ ] In unit not previously certified [ ] In unit previously certified in Case No. _____ .

[ ] AC-AMENDMENT OF CERTIFICATION—Petitioner seeks amendment of certification issued in Case No. _____ .

Attach statement describing the specific amendment sought.

2. NAME OF EMPLOYER	EMPLOYER REPRESENTATIVE TO CONTACT	PHONE NO
XYZ Manufacturing Co.	John Hancock	222-2222

3. ADDRESS(ES) OF ESTABLISHMENT(S) INVOLVED *(Street and number. city. State. and ZIP Code)*
P.O. Box 100, Boston, Massachusetts

4a. TYPE OF ESTABLISHMENT *(Factory. mine. wholesaler. etc.)*	4b. IDENTIFY PRINCIPAL PRODUCT OR SERVICE
Manufacturing	Metal Specialties

5. Unit Involved *(In UC petition. describe PRESENT bargaining unit and attach description of proposed clarification.)*

	6a. NUMBER OF EMPLOYEES IN UNIT
Included: All production and maintenance employees	PRESENT about 200
	PROPOSED (BY UC/AC)
Excluded: Office clerical employees, professional employees, guards and/or watchmen, and supervisors as defined in the Act.	6b. IS THIS PETITION SUPPORTED BY 30% OR MORE OF THE EMPLOYEES IN THE UNIT?* [X] YES [ ] NO *Not applicable in R.M. UC. and AC

(If you have checked box RC in 1 above. check and complete EITHER item 7a or 7b. whichever is applicable)

7a. [ ] Request for recognition as Bargaining Representative was made on _____ *(Month. day. year)* and Employer declined recognition on or about _____ *(Month. day. year)* *(If no reply received. so state)*

7b. [ ] Petitioner is currently recognized as Bargaining Representative and desires certification under the act.

8. Recognized or Certified Bargaining Agent *(If there is none. so state)*

NAME None	AFFILIATION
ADDRESS	DATE OF RECOGNITION OR CERTIFICATION

9. DATE OF EXPIRATION OF CURRENT CONTRACT, IF ANY *(Show month. day. and year)* None	10. IF YOU HAVE CHECKED BOX UD IN 1 ABOVE, SHOW HERE THE DATE OF EXECUTION OF AGREEMENT GRANTING UNION SHOP *(Month. day. and year)*

11a. IS THERE NOW A STRIKE OR PICKETING AT THE EMPLOYER'S ESTABLISHMENT(S) INVOLVED? YES _____ NO X	11b. IF SO, APPROXIMATELY HOW MANY EMPLOYEES ARE PARTICIPATING?

11c. THE EMPLOYER HAS BEEN PICKETED BY OR ON BEHALF OF _____ *(Insert name)* , A LABOR ORGANIZATION, OF _____ *(Insert address)* SINCE _____ *(Month. day. year)*

12. ORGANIZATIONS OR INDIVIDUALS OTHER THAN PETITIONER (AND OTHER THAN THOSE NAMED IN ITEMS 8 AND 11c), WHICH HAVE CLAIMED RECOGNITION AS REPRESENTATIVES AND OTHER ORGANIZATIONS AND INDIVIDUALS KNOWN TO HAVE A REPRESENTATIVE INTEREST IN ANY EMPLOYEES IN THE UNIT DESCRIBED IN ITEM 5 ABOVE. (IF NONE, SO STATE.)

NAME	AFFILIATION	ADDRESS	DATE OF CLAIM *(Required only if Petition is filed by Employer)*

I declare that I have read the above petition and that the statements therein are true to the best of my knowledge and belief.

XYZ Employees Association
(Petitioner and affiliation. if any)

By s/John Doe
(Signature of representative or person filing petition) An Individual *(Title. if any)*

Address 1000 East 100th Street, Boston, Massachusetts 333-3333
(Street and number city. State. and ZIP Code) *(Telephone number)*

WILLFULLY FALSE STATEMENT ON THIS PETITION CAN BE PUNISHED BY FINE AND IMPRISONMENT (U.S. CODE, TITLE 18, SECTION 1001)

GPO 894-283

PETITION FOR DECERTIFICATION ELECTION

Form NLRB-502
(11-64)

UNITED STATES OF AMERICA
NATIONAL LABOR RELATIONS BOARD

PETITION

Form Approved.
Budget Bureau No. 64-R002.14

DO NOT WRITE IN THIS SPACE

CASE NO.

INSTRUCTIONS.—Submit an original and four (4) copies of this Petition to the NLRB Regional Office in the Region in which the employer concerned is located. If more space is required for any one item, attach additional sheets, numbering item accordingly.

DATE FILED

The Petitioner alleges that the following circumstances exist and requests that the National Labor Relations Board proceed under its proper authority pursuant to Section 9 of the National Labor Relations Act.

1. Purpose of this Petition *(If box RC, RM, or RD is checked and a charge under Section 8(b)(7) of the Act has been filed involving the Employer named herein, the statement following the description of the type of petition shall not be deemed made.)*

(Check one)

☐ RC-CERTIFICATION OF REPRESENTATIVES—A substantial number of employees wish to be represented for purposes of collective bargaining by Petitioner and Petitioner desires to be certified as representative of the employees.

☐ RM-REPRESENTATION (EMPLOYER PETITION)—One or more individuals or labor organizations have presented a claim to Petitioner to be recognized as the representative of employees of Petitioner.

☒ RD-DECERTIFICATION — A substantial number of employees assert that the certified or currently recognized bargaining representative is no longer their representative.

☐ UD-WITHDRAWAL OF UNION SHOP AUTHORITY—Thirty percent (30%) or more of employees in a bargaining unit covered by an agreement between their employer and a labor organization desire that such authority be rescinded.

☐ UC-UNIT CLARIFICATION—A labor organization is currently recognized by employer, but petitioner seeks clarification of placement of certain employees: *(Check one)* ☐ In unit not previously certified
☐ In unit previously certified in Case No. _____

☐ AC-AMENDMENT OF CERTIFICATION—Petitioner seeks amendment of certification issued in Case No. _____

Attach statement describing the specific amendment sought.

2. NAME OF EMPLOYER	EMPLOYER REPRESENTATIVE TO CONTACT	PHONE NO.
XYZ Manufacturing Co.	John Henry	222-2222

3. ADDRESS(ES) OF ESTABLISHMENT(S) INVOLVED *(Street and number, city, State, and ZIP Code)*

P.O. Box 100, Boston, Massachusetts

4a. TYPE OF ESTABLISHMENT *(Factory, mine, wholesaler, etc.)*	4b. IDENTIFY PRINCIPAL PRODUCT OR SERVICE
Manufacturing	Metal Specialties

5. Unit Involved *(In UC petition, describe PRESENT bargaining unit and attach description of proposed clarification.)*

Included

All production and maintenance employees

Excluded

Office clerical employees, professional employees, guards and/or watchmen, and supervisors as defined in the Act.

6a. NUMBER OF EMPLOYEES IN UNIT.

PRESENT about 200

PROPOSED (BY UC/AC)

6b. IS THIS PETITION SUPPORTED BY 30% OR MORE OF THE EMPLOYEES IN THE UNIT?*

☒ YES ☐ NO

*Not applicable in RM, UC, and AC

(If you have checked box RC in 1 above, check and complete EITHER item 7a or 7b, whichever is applicable)

7a. ☐ Request for recognition as Bargaining Representative was made on .... *(Month, day, year)* .... and Employer

declined recognition on or about .... *(Month, day, year)* *(If no reply received, so state)*

7b. ☐ Petitioner is currently recognized as Bargaining Representative and desires certification under the act.

8. Recognized or Certified Bargaining Agent *(If there is none, so state)*

NAME	AFFILIATION
XYZ Employees Association	Independent
ADDRESS	DATE OF RECOGNITION OR CERTIFICATION
1000 East 100th Street, Boston, Massachusetts	January 28, 1972

9. DATE OF EXPIRATION OF CURRENT CONTRACT, IF ANY *(Show month, day, and year)*	10. IF YOU HAVE CHECKED BOX UD IN 1 ABOVE, SHOW HERE THE DATE OF EXECUTION OF AGREEMENT GRANTING UNION SHOP *(Month, day, and year)*
None	

11a. IS THERE NOW A STRIKE OR PICKETING AT THE EMPLOYER'S ESTABLISHMENT(S) INVOLVED? YES .... NO X	11b. IF SO, APPROXIMATELY HOW MANY EMPLOYEES ARE PARTICIPATING?

11c. THE EMPLOYER HAS BEEN PICKETED BY OR ON BEHALF OF .... *(Insert name)* .... A LABOR

ORGANIZATION, OF .... *(Insert address)* .... SINCE .... *(Month, day, year)*

12. ORGANIZATIONS OR INDIVIDUALS OTHER THAN PETITIONER (AND OTHER THAN THOSE NAMED IN ITEMS 8 AND 11c), WHICH HAVE CLAIMED RECOGNITION AS REPRESENTATIVES AND OTHER ORGANIZATIONS AND INDIVIDUALS KNOWN TO HAVE A REPRESENTATIVE INTEREST IN ANY EMPLOYEES IN THE UNIT DESCRIBED IN ITEM 5 ABOVE. (IF NONE, SO STATE.)

NAME	AFFILIATION	ADDRESS	DATE OF CLAIM *(Required only if Petition is filed by Employer)*

I declare that I have read the above petition and that the statements therein are true to the best of my knowledge and belief.

Bill Smith
(Petitioner and affiliation, if any)

By s/Bill Smith
(Signature of representative or person filing petition)

An Individual
(Title, if any)

Address 101 East 10th Street, Boston, Massachusetts
(Street and number, city, State, and ZIP Code)

123-4567
(Telephone number)

WILLFULLY FALSE STATEMENT ON THIS PETITION CAN BE PUNISHED BY FINE AND IMPRISONMENT (U.S. CODE, TITLE 18, SECTION 1001)

GPO 894-283

AUTHORIZATION

I hereby designate and authorize the XYZ Employees Association as my collective bargaining agent in all matters pertaining to wages, hours, and other terms and conditions of employment.

Date	Signature
	Address
	City State Zip

UNITED STATES OF AMERICA

National Labor Relations Board

OFFICIAL SECRET BALLOT

SPECIMEN

FOR CERTAIN EMPLOYEES OF
XYZ Manufacturing Co.
Boston, Massachusetts

Do you wish to be represented for purposes of collective bargaining by -

XYZ Employees Association

MARK AN "X" IN THE SQUARE OF YOUR CHOICE

YES

NO

DO NOT SIGN THIS BALLOT. Fold and drop in ballot box.
If you spoil this ballot return it to the Board Agent for a new one.

SUGGESTED READINGS

Listed below are some of the books or pamphlets which you will find helpful if you want to learn more about labor relations. They are easy to read.

Arbitration and Labor Relations, by Clarence M. Updegroff, published by the Bureau of National Affairs, Inc., 1231 – 25th St. N.W., Washington, D.C. 20037. 454 pages, $12.50 (Third Ed., 1970).

Basic Patterns in Union Contracts, published by the Bureau of National Affairs, Inc., 1231 – 25th St. N.W., Washington, D.C. 20037. About 52 pages, paperback, $5.00 (Seventh Ed., 1971).

The Job Safety and Health Act of 1970, published by the Bureau of National Affairs, Inc., 1231 – 25th St. N.W., Washington, D.C. 20037. 342 pages, $15.00 (1971).

Labor Law Handbook, by Wesley M. Wilson, published by Bobbs-Merrill Co., 4300 W. 62nd Ave., Indianapolis, Indiana 46206 (1963). 518 pages plus cumulative pocket supplement, about 144 pages, $17.50 with supplement.

The 1972 Civil Rights Law and Your Business, published by Prentice-Hall, Inc., Dept. S-L-CR-103, Englewood Cliffs, New Jersey 07632. 48 pages, paperback, $1.75 (1972).

The following booklets with paper covers are available from the Superintendent of Documents, U.S. Government Printing Office, Washington, D.C. 20402.

Brief History of the American Labor Movement, Catalog No. L2.3: 1000/4 S/N 2901-0388, $1.00 (1970).

Growth of Labor Law in the United States, Catalog No. L1.2:L 41/967, about 311 pages, $1.25 (1967).